Global Environment of Contemporary Public Action

Global Environment of Contemporary Public Action

Walter Gérard AMEDZRO ST-HILAIRE, Ph.D.

NorthAmerican
Business Press
Atlanta – Seattle – South Florida - Toronto

North American Business Press, Inc.
Atlanta, Georgia
Seattle, Washington
South Florida
Toronto, Canada

Global Environment of Contemporary Public Action
ISBN: 978-0-9828434-9-9

Cover art by Camp Pope Publishing.

Library of Congress Control Number 2011934662

Library of Congress
Cataloging in Publication Division
101 Independence Ave., SE
Washington, DC 20540-4320
Printed in the United States of America
First Edition: 978-0-9828434-9-9

ABOUT THE AUTHOR

Walter Gérard AMEDZRO ST-HILAIRE, Ph.D., is a research leader. His specializations include public finances, governance, strategic management, and international expertise. He has several years of academic experience to his credit having taught public finance, operations, and strategic management courses, as well as research methods in organization studies, and systems analysis and design in various universities.

Aside from his research and teaching engagements, Dr. AMEDZRO ST-HILAIRE is project manager and business Analyst for a lot of African crown corporations. As part of his contributions to the academic community, he has researched and written extensively on corporate governance and some of his contributions have been published in peer-reviewed journals and in various conference proceedings.

Proud holder of several postdoctoral awards, Dr. Walter Gérard AMEDZRO ST-HILAIRE directs the prestigious Global Journal of Strategies & Governance.

TABLE OF CONTENTS

INTRODUCTION

Globalization of the economy is not a recent phenomenon: over the centuries, increased trade, movement of ideas and people, dissemination of knowledge, skills and techniques, such as computer, has gradually opened up economies and borders.

However, the dramatic acceleration of this process, witnessed since the eighties, forced the industrialized countries to a sudden and recent awareness of a trend, seen in as both a test to undergo and a challenge to take on.

This has led to numerous, if contradictory, analyses and comments by both politicians and economists, as the march towards globalization has profoundly altered the global balance, questioning the traditional development pattern between rich and poor countries. But this break from historical precedent, embodied in the significant annual growth rate recorded in certain countries, long defined as "developing", and the economic ultra-growth of Southeastern Asia, is fueling concerns and uncertainties. Thus, this confrontation between the poor enriching themselves and rich nations seemingly becoming poorer inevitably leads to theories arguing that the first factor is a cause of the second.

So, while, Southeastern Asian average growth of the next twenty years could reach 7.5% per year, the recent financial crisis has disrupted global economic development. Nonetheless, after an initial panic reaction subsequent analyses give hope of less change than first feared.

However, this crisis' consequences are real even though adverse effects were limited to only certain geographical areas. In this regard, it darkens any long-term prospects for the world economy and public policies, not only, by undermining the current economic starting point, but also by leaving heavy uncertainties about an eventual sustainable restart of the global economic system.

From a cyclical point of view, although it is clear that this global crisis lead, in the short run to a weak economic recovery, one needs to embrace the idea that the current economic system is flexible enough to support the recovery.

It would therefore be wise to lay down strict rules to standardize public budgets and monetary policies. The recent trend to financial deregulation has adversely affected public budgets, in effect the monetary policy rules themselves were altered.

A current major lesson is that economic growth is a fundamental element of social pacts and that priority should be given to a return to this concept. Equally, it is essential to make such a change before the current financial problems spread from the financial sphere to the real economy and results in a decline in real activity, measured in thousands of job cuts.

The explosion of deficits and, furthermore, public liabilities inflation, as a consequence of the global financial system's rescue, have profoundly affected public finances benchmarks. Orders of magnitude, whether in loss of market value and wealth or in the scope of plans to address the crisis, have changed scale: deficits accrue, states' debt swells as ever and yet the burdens appear to grow.

At the moment and for the immediate future, Governments are, in terms of interest rates, "in the eye of the storm": they are refinanced on average at historical lows. But one will have to be well aware that, so far, the major industrial states have found the resources they needed to finance their operations, through the abundance of liquidity accumulated in recent years and, especially, by massive central banks' interventions.

Certainly, one should not exclude at global level, a Japanese-style scenario in which continuing problems in the banking system would permanently stifle growth. However, even in a gradual recovery context, we cannot eliminate the risk of a new kind of negative interaction between financial and real economy. Sooner or later, the issue of Governments' solvency will arise again to establish a new hierarchy between countries based on the sustainability of their public finances and, more generally, of their business model: the sooner they will feel a sort of "normalcy", the sooner they will be able to move away from government securities to those issued by companies, risking a credit crunch, even a bond market crash. This hardly seems topical: global economic powers' finances still appear solid, while no sign of change is perceived in the direction of the issuing institutions' monetary policies.

Yet central banks will have to withdraw the injected cash and reduce balance sheets overly inflated by interventions to ensure continued funding of the economy at some stage. Is this really the major challenge facing central bankers who will be responsible for organizing the reflux without creating disturbances in nature?

In addition, could improving the global economic situation, paradoxically, not lead to increased tensions in the most vulnerable countries as in the system as a whole? The author argues that there is potential for additional financial shocks, especially if fears of the resurgence of inflation leads central banks to relax their monetary policies, in such a way as to create patterns of a checkered global recovery ("W"). While immediate financial constraints are hardly felt, as it seems, because some currencies remain strong and the exceptional market conditions based on the comfort of existing "deficits", difficult decisions obviously need to be taken. This sustainability of the global economic model remains in doubt and under constant evaluation by the markets. This is the major focus of the analyses presented in this book, which relevantly identifies public finance models in industrialized countries in crisis while setting out, on the one hand, desirable economic and administrative reforms and, on the other hand, new trends will impact on international governance initiatives.

PART ONE

Hinges of the New Global Economic Deal: Offshoring and Need to Renew Industrial Policies

CHAPTER 1

An Analysis of Offshoring Phenomenon: A Debate Tending to Appeasement

Offshoring is a generic term with confusing definitions that has become synonymous with job destruction. Offshoring has accompanied and probably amplified the effects of economic globalization. In this respect, to understand contemporary global governance and its relevance to the socio-economic and financial crisis it is critical to first study this key element of the new global business environment.

In fact, facilitated by lower transport costs and modern telecommunications, it has affected easily transportable, compact products such as textiles, footwear, toys, and, more recently software, and other technology products and services that can rely on the modern ICT environment such as accounting, and clerical work..

The acceleration of manufacturing sites' movement from rich to poor countries, the direct effect it produces on the job – including the less skilled – have been frequently raised. Over the past few years, the examination of the offshoring phenomenon has led to multiple analyses, as passionate as they are divergent. Some saw this as a logical and inevitable evolution towards a new distribution of jobs in the world: unskilled labor industries locating in new rich countries while the most advanced nations keep their technological advance and promote the opening of new overseas markets enabled by the displacement of employment.

Others have seen, conversely, that this unskilled jobs loss drove the countries' economy into bankruptcy and that a more protectionist model was the only viable outcome. Some have attributed to offshoring the loss of thousands of jobs, the others have argued that they have instead helped to safeguard some of the jobs that would have been lost anyway.

These various analyses all have their share of the truth: there is no doubt that some traditional industries have been wiped out by competition from emerging countries. But at the same time, these Governments positioned themselves as new markets whose considerable potential for development offers great opportunities for manufacturers. In effect it is not one sided as the relocation of industry has also created new markets and the share of Asian countries' imports in world trade has multiplied by six and Chinese imports more than tripled in value since 1998.

Such prospects motivate industrialists to prepare to meet this demand, usually by locating in these countries the means and tools of production. In this sense, there is no alternative investment benefitting foreign countries; on the contrary, these relocations condition the investor sector's future growth.

Multiple studies recently conducted on these foreign investments issues indicate that offshoring is a consequence rather than just a cause, of globalization and the most recent reviews appear to be moving towards a more optimistic view of the global economy. There has been, recently, but significantly, a perceptible reconciliation between defenders and opponents of globalization. Growth return in industrialized countries has probably a lot to do with this peace: indeed, this part of the world emerged from a period of strong dispersion of national circumstances and poor average performance.

It is my contention that globalization does not destroy jobs, since growth and employment in the West depends on their relations with the net importing countries. Globalization must become the true growth engine in the next few years.

Once this evolution of the trading rules is accepted as inevitable, countries cannot simply endure it: they must find ways of adapting so as to maintain and develop the industry on their territory.

Indeed, industry and public finances in some countries found themselves quickly confronted with the globalization of the economy, which has had negative effects, creating an increasingly fierce international competition, and positive effects, allowing new markets to open. This double impact can only grow stronger in the future. Since many industries' survival depends on the ability to ensure their place in the world, it is impossible to yield to any protectionist temptation. But neither is it possible to give in without control or reason to extensive free trade.

CHAPTER 2

The Need for an Enhanced Economic Policy

To ensure an economic adjustment and maintain healthy public finances, it is imperative to develop new industrial strengths and not to see deindustrialization as the only option. Industry must remain at the core of economic policy and its capacity to export is the simplest solution to the end of global economic and financial crisis.

A. The industry-services opposition: an outdated debate

In the constant battle waged by countries against unemployment, industry's importance has probably been underestimated, particularly in developed economies where there has been a tendency to assume the tertiary sector to be the best – even the only – method of fostering job creation.

Admittedly, the services sector accounts for more jobs than industry and agriculture combined: over the last fifteen years, 118 million jobs were created in the tertiary sector in total; meanwhile, 13 million jobs were lost in agriculture and industry. But industry is essential to maintaining overall employment: a job created in industry is at least two jobs created in services, it is said, and it cannot reasonably be expected to have a strong economy without a strong industrial base.

Encouraging industry is the same as promoting economic power and employment. It is not possible to replace industrial jobs by those in services sector because there can be no sustainable service sector without industry. One should not forget that service activity remains dependent on industrial activity, with, for example, about from 30% to 40% for service jobs related to goods exports. It is thus estimated that about 2.5 million people work, in some emerging powers, in the businesses service sector.

Moreover, distinguishing between industrial employment and service employment is a difficult undertaking. In part, this is due to the extent a given firm indulges in outsourcing: so for example, industrial facilities' maintenance jobs may be counted as manufacturing jobs if done within the company, but as service activities if contracted with a cleaning company. The boundaries can therefore be artificial, especially around the separation between secondary and tertiary sectors.

B. The urgency of a relevant economic policy

Emerging countries need an industrial policy to meet their legitimate ambitions. If this need is clear, the process is not simple in part because of ideological differences.

Indeed, unlike their main competitors, the American and European industrialized countries, the other candidates for global economic power have the greatest difficulty speaking with one voice. They accumulate disability, include several jurisdictions, are consumerist and are not protectionist. The diversity of economic beliefs animating the governments then leads them to react in spurts, depending on events. They may thus opt for an over-rigid application of competition rules and lose sight of all industrial purpose.

Conversely, it can also select the industry, in violation of competition principles. This constant oscillation between industry and competition needs to be resolved if these Governments aim to definitely join the global economic elite. It is time to seize the opportunity presented by economic growth return and easing of the western capitalist financial crisis' effects.

The second problem is that there can be no return to an outdated approach to politics, resulting in increased governmental intervention in the economic sector. In the past, moreover, this has not always led to the expected results. Neither can protectionism be used to protect their market in order to postpone the necessary adjustments and technical changes. Candidates for global economic governance must understand that competition is an asset.

Certainly, we will not invent a new industrial policy today. But the powerful economies of the world can implement with determination, a range of, competitive, commercial and industrial budget strategies, which will create an environment conducive to economic recovery in a world that will, with or without them, be more and more globalized.

PART TWO

The Nature of the Post-Global Crisis in Perspective

CHAPTER 3

The Nature of the Crisis: Structural or Cyclical?

No sustainable plan for the global economy prospect can be constructed without serious reflection on the international context. As we have seen the contemporary economy is completely immersed in globalization, and, in consequence, has not escaped the global crisis effects which led to a historic decline in production levels. In this regard the next quarter century is at stake and this leads, undoubtedly, to fundamental questions about the future. Beyond financial imbalances and their effects on the real economy, the primary problems are failures manifested in the real economy.

A macroeconomic system was implemented on a global scale, accompanied by unprecedented financial cash flows that led to a global system that has not been adequately controlled. This makes the crisis not just about cyclical policies. Countries' growth schemes, that is to say their respective economic engines, are incompatible, or create, at least at the international level, a sub-optimal situation.

- From a cyclical point of view, the crisis has reversed the decoupling theory, since the difficulties encountered in the U.S. were quickly transmitted to the world economy as a whole; this reinforces the need for common and consistent responses to impacts, even, if possible, a reflection on crisis prevention, at the global level.
- From a structural standpoint, the crisis is interpreted as the result of imbalances arising from a discrepancy between the major world economies' growth patterns. The apparent complementarity of national economies (e.g. complementarity between savings and Asian American consumer) should not obscure the factors of tension and the risk of crisis engendered by global imbalances. Lack of coordination is even more damaging when the monetary framework is common.

A. An uncertain recovery

I. A unique global recession

The financial crisis is the worst global recession since 1929. During its second year's first quarter, global activity has slowed. On this whole year, world trade has shrunk of 12.5%.

The crisis began with the U.S. subprime mortgage market, in effect as a debt crisis: excessive credit growth was based, in previous years, on the prospect of rapid increases in assets, including in real estate. This housing bubble and credit bubble fed each other. The easing of credit conditions, combined with risk dilution through securitization, created an unstable system that collapsed during the U.S. housing market downturn.

Two factors that worsened the financial crisis came together:

- On one hand, interdependence between different asset markets;
- On the other hand, a weakening of the banking system.

These two factors have catalyzed the financial crisis that was rapidly transmitted to the real economy, through the usual shock transmission channels between financial and real economy:

- bank asset depreciation encouraged financial institutions to restrict access to credit for households and businesses, resulting negatively in terms of consumption and investment;
- the collapse of financial markets resulted in negative wealth effects that have impacted the overall demand. These contagion effects have been compounded by a widespread trust breakdown of businesses and households, faced with the necessity of debt relief.

Signs of recovery have emerged, however, by mid-2009.

II. A painstaking recovery

Governments have established strong stimulus, and provided the financial system with guarantees, which helped restore confidence. Central banks have responded to the crisis by lowering interest rates to historically low levels. Besides lower rates, central banks have intervened by massively injecting liquidity, to replace the now faulty interbank markets. The crisis forced them to adopt so-called non-conventional policies, leading to an expansion and a change in the nature of their balance sheets. The second half of the second year following the crisis saw activity pick up, thanks to a strong rebound in China, which has contributed to the stabilization of activity in advanced countries.

The reversal of the inventory cycle has also positively influenced the activity, the end of destocking resulting mechanically in production restarting due to renewed orders. The economic recovery will not suffice to halt the continuing unemployment rise. The average unemployment rate is expected to stabilize slightly below 5% in 2011, while close to 9% elsewhere.

1. Unemployment trend forecast in the world

The evolution of employment differs by country: in United States, employment adjustment has been very rapid, with an unemployment rate rising by 4 points; in Germany, however, unemployment increased by less than 1 point, resulting in a decrease in per capita productivity, offset by an increase in hourly productivity (due to the decline in hours worked per worker) as a result of partial unemployment. Major G7 countries' labor markets have reacted differently to the crisis. Under the effect of working time reduction, productivity per capita decline has occurred, partly offset by an increase in hourly productivity. In most economies, the average weekly hours worked has decreased, due to the strengthening of partial unemployment benefits programs, and in connection with particularly strong crisis effects on manufacturing and construction, which are two sectors where working time is more sensitive to the cycle.

Schematically, while job losses were limited in continental Europe by reducing the working time, they were, however, very numerous in the United States as a result of more rapid adjustment to activity changes. Evolution is generally symmetrical during upturns, employment picking up more quickly in countries where the adjustments were more abrupt. But there is no automaticity in this process and there is a difficult debate in America concerning the rate of recovery in employment. Moreover, despite the upturn in activity, employment continued to shrink. Although unemployment seems to have stabilized, in theory it should continue to rise, as the cyclical decline in labor force alone allows amortizing this increase. More generally, demand increase ran up last year against weakened consumption and external demand contribution. This recovery could therefore be only a technical interlude related to the end of companies destocking.

In total, the factors that have supported recent economic activity tend to run out, whether economic policies or end of destocking. Meanwhile, crisis recessionary effects, the need to clean up banks' balance sheets, and rising unemployment seem to have to have more influence on the underlying growth prospects than would be consistent with a strong and rapid economic recovery. The assumption of a recovery followed by a new recession has not disappeared. Fiscal stances of individual countries needs to address this as poorly controlled disturbances on sovereign debt markets are likely to destabilize them, exacerbating the already heavy existing macroeconomic risks.

B. A crisis with structural imbalance

The current crisis does not reveal a new world: it is instead a reflection of today's world's pathologies. These pathologies were not erased by the crisis, which suggests delayed or ongoing chronic effects if the coordination between actors is not strengthened as part of enhanced regional and global governance.

I. An unregulated abundance of cash

The crisis results from a combination of macro and microeconomic factors that led to the emergence of speculative bubbles on certain assets. It is even more urgent to address, at the international level, the macro-and micro-prudential regulation issue since responses to the crisis have further increased the liquidity level in the global economy.

1. Global liquidity excess

From a macroeconomic perspective, the credibility that central banks gained in the years preceding the crisis led to a significant increase in the money supply without inflationary pressures. The ratio of money supply in the strict sense and GDP, for industrialized countries, thus increased from about 20% over a period of 20 years to over 26% 7 years ago, reaching nearly 30% 5 years ago.

Meanwhile, global inflation has been decreasing. Decreasing interest rates and risk premiums fueled credit expansion and rising asset prices, in a context of strong global growth:

- stock prices rose sharply from 1997 to 2000, then from 2003 to 2007;
- real estate prices soared between 2000 and 2005;
- commodity prices have also increased sharply between 2002 and 2008.

Yet macroeconomic policymakers' responses to the crisis now contribute to increased liquidity. After the sharp decline in certain assets prices, this could contribute to new speculative sequences generating further instability.

II. Unbalanced growth schemes

Excessive private debt was a not particularly studied before the crisis, the emphasis instead being placed on public accounts imbalances and balance of payments issues. However, private debt increase is symptomatic of underlying problems.

1. *A mismatch between supply and demand plans...*

In addition to issues specific to financial markets operation, whose efficiency has been radically challenged by the crisis, the excessive private debt raises, at the real economy level, the question of matching supply and demand schemes, leading us to meditate on value added distribution and increased wages dispersion.

Businesses' margin rate, which represents the profits share (EBITDA) in value added terms, increased significantly in the U.S. and, over the last ten years, in the UK. On the other hand, it has been stable in other industrialized states since the 1990s where the profit share amounts to about one-third of the value added.

However, these governments suffered, as elsewhere, widening inequality, which fuels a sense of unequal sharing of growth fruits. The incomes of the richest grew much faster than average in Canada, because of the strong unearned income increase and the rise in the highest salaries.

This high incomes explosion is mainly concentrated in the top percentile of households, whose share in total income increased significantly in the last 10 years. In particular, households in higher income percentile saw their real income grow by 40.9% over the period, against 4.5% for 92% of households within the first income brackets. In United States, the bulk of income growth has been captured by the richest one percent. At the other end of the social ladder, the less skilled workers have suffered from increased flexibility of the production system. It seems, at least in the U.S., the UK and Spain, that credit has been a means to address the growing inequality in a context where consumption was the main engine of a group of economies largely dependent on household demand and whose growth rate had become, in fact, higher than its potential and higher than in most G8 countries.

This is one of the explanations given to increasing households' indebtedness in the country concerned. U.S. households' debt has, for example, increased particularly quickly, outstanding financial commitments increasing from 89% to 192% of their disposable income over the past 10 years. In view of U.S. households, Canadian households seem generally under-indebted, partly due to the institutional and regulatory framework. Nevertheless, consumer loans have increased significantly faster than loans to individual entrepreneurs (but more slowly than home loans over the same period) so that Canadian household debt equivalent in disposable income has increased significantly.

III. Suboptimal growth schemes

In addition to their internal imbalances, the major world economies' growth patterns show signs of inconsistency leading to a sub-optimal economic situation, at the global level, as a result of the lack of coordination in macro-economic policies.

1. At the global level

Global imbalances, particularly United States' external deficit and China's surpluses, were substantially reduced during the recession. However, this adjustment now looks complete and imbalances remain at high levels. The risk of a severe exchange rates adjustment exists, which argues for greater coordination within the G20.

2. At the regional level

The coordination problem is a major issue within the G8, with their different and sometimes antagonistic growth patterns. Canadian growth is indeed based more on household consumption, while growth in the U.S. is dependent on external competitiveness gains, boosted by a wage policy of competitive disinflation. This type of discrepancy leads to "losers-losers" strategies in the long term.

CHAPTER 4

A Sharp Deterioration in Public Finances

The evolution of public finances pre-crisis appeared to show improved accounting balance drawing prospects of a reduction of public debt weight in GDP, with the possible exception of the costs related to growing longevity. In this scenario, some countries were faced with situations considered particularly favorable while others were tardy in adjusting their public accounts.

As an example, the model of financial supervision established in Canada expressed an overall good report considering the changing public finances structure. The latter, seen through public balances' components analysis - structural and cyclical - has proven inadequate to make an adequate structural diagnosis. The questions raised by growth patterns sustainability, underlying the public finances evolution have been too much neglected.

Under these conditions, the appearance of financial strength in some governments backfired when the crisis came. Imbalances in public accounts widened, undermining the balance achieved that had implied a controlled public debt evolution. It is often countries in the most favorable positions that found themselves in the worst financial situations.

These observations highlight two challenges for the future:

- The first is to build an economically and financially realistic oversight of public finances, which involves paying deserved attention to the sustainability of growth patterns;
- The second is more fundamental: it is to establish economic growth patterns that do not respond to financial crises in order to preserve public finances from the shocks they bring.

The second challenge is fraught with the challenges inherent to designing fiscal policy: this should be configured so that it is able to exert its insurance effects when macroeconomic and financial crises trigger. Instead of just designing fiscal policy on a cyclical balancing basis, and not upsetting other objectives - public goods production and redistribution -, such a policy now needs to solve structural imbalances in economic growth patterns..

A. The pre-crisis: a smokescreen improvement in fiscal positions

I. Improved fiscal positions, but a relatively large deficit

At the end of the first year of the crisis, the balance of the majority of industrialized countries appeared weakened in regard to the generally observed trends in the years before this crisis.

G20's average position in terms of deficit had more than doubled. The United States was the country the most in deficit, its deficit higher than its northern neighbor's. The situation in some countries, however, was less bad, when assessed using the structural balance that can capture more accurately public accounts' balance as it offsets the effects of the cycle on the fiscal position alone.

While the nominal deficit averaged in the G8 was more than four times G20 countries' average deficit, the structural deficit was on average only twice higher than the same observed deficit. In other words, for a large part, the "superiority" of other industrialized nations' fiscal performance emerged as cyclical, that is to say, unsustainable. For example, while G8 knew a near balance of its net public vote, it recorded a significantly less favorable structural balance.

However, the situation generally shared by industrialized countries of having a structural balance less positive than the nominal position was the same as others with a gap between the two balances of the same order.

II. The deficiencies of fiscal positions supervision

1. General comments

Financial supervision is provided in most G7 countries by the national budget authorities and rating agencies, who draw together a range of indicators. It is important in this context to remember in particular that:

- The public deficit level reached by the countries had never been so low since the early 1970s;
- While many countries were under prohibitive budgetary surveillance, only a few even knew that.
- Finally, public finances long-term sustainability was strengthened, most countries having reduced the "sustainability gap" in public finances.

In this view, only the situations of some countries were considered a cause for concern. However, an additional reservation was the strength of fiscal adjustment with the question of the structural deficit's true level generally in industrialized countries, especially in light of changing public expenditure. Regarding the prescriptive component, it is useful highlight the related uncertainties on economic activity by estimating that, if some government could use their structural budget position to allow automatic stabilizers, others, which had not yet reached their medium-term budgetary target, should continue on the structural adjustment path. These countries should allow such stabilizers only in this limit, while respecting, in any event, a public deficit ceiling.

2. *An inadequate budget monitoring*

Budget monitoring and fiscal policy analysis are based on concepts that require careful presentation especially as these terms are not always used accurately. The distinction between structural and cyclical fiscal stances occupies a prominent place in the budget analysis, which has, in most cases, a legal status since it refers explicitly to laws and regulations. Even so there are enforcement problems, which should be highlighted, not just to highlight an important technical point, but to improve its relevance.

Moreover, and this is an important issue for the future, budget monitoring should be supplemented to take into account the need for balance between growth regimes and the budgetary supervision instruments.

i. *General issues of monitoring public finances' structural position*

The goal is to somehow avoid the illusions arising from a simplistic budget nominalism to appreciate what a balanced budget draws from unsustainable circumstances. Public revenues and expenditures which are its two key components are sensitive to economic activity. The key issue is to understand if these remain in balance despite short term variations in economic activity.

This seemingly simple correction raises significant issues, some technical, others more fundamental, related to difficulties in estimating potential growth rates. Technically, the assessment of public finances' structural position is disturbed by a series of choices regarding, first, public revenues processing. The main problem is the fate of tax revenues resulting from non-unitary elasticity: should they be included in the structural balance calculation or consider them as cyclical? One could add the interest expenditures processing issue. The total expenses variation related to changes in interest payments on public debt is seen as impacting the structural balance. This choice is not obvious if one considers the level of interest rates as more or less consistent with interest rate equilibrium. It would be, in this case, justified to allocate a portion of public debt interest to the cyclical component of government balance and the other to its structural component.

These technical issues are not without significant practical extensions. In times of bubbles, the tax bases used for certain statutory charges take values conducive to dynamism of public revenue exceeding what economic growth alone suggests. From this perspective, the period before crisis onset illustrates the problems created by a method that fails to make sufficient reference to perennial fiscal developments. Without this explanation neither being exclusive, nor even the most decisive, there are real difficulties in assessing an adequate budgetary position in industrialized countries.

Beyond these methodological issues, estimating the structural situation of public accounts balances leads to the fundamental problem of assessing potential growth. A particular problem over the long term is that an error of 0.1 percentage points of GDP per year is more than 6 points of value added in volume over 15 years. In sum, budgetary positions analysis based on the distinction between structural and cyclical fiscal stance is not the sole basis on which to assess the soundness of budgetary positions.

ii. Strengthening budgetary positions' economic analysis

The assumptions made on average by industrialized countries on the eve of the economic and financial crisis, which would result in a profound deterioration in public finances, were rather favorable. Less than a year later, government finances imbalances averaged a historically unprecedented level. One might consider that their degradation comes from an essentially unpredictable accident. But there is also reason to emphasize that imbalances in the economy, whether international, with trade balances, or domestic, with the money supply drift and, in some countries, higher asset prices, had been discussed and should have been considered.

In this respect, let us show the inverse relationship between public and private debt level to show that, under an unbalanced growth scheme, there is a kind of trade-off between the two debts. Similarly, that trade imbalances' magnitude, should be highlighted along with their root cause: in other words, the inconsistency, or even antagonism, of growth schemes adopted by individual countries. In effect this calls attention to the importance of growth patterns in the budgetary oversight.

Theoretically, the major industrialized countries of the world should be able to present their medium term budgets consistent with a macroeconomic scenario that represents the underlying situation. However, in fact, macroeconomic trajectories analysis - which creates budget scenarios - appeared too brief in many of these countries, these trajectories' consistency with the fiscal stances not being the less weak link of this analysis.

It should be noted that the analysis of the economic situation remained characterized in all developed countries by superficial recognition of links between budgetary positions and the economic activity reality, and a questionable assumption of independence between countries' fiscal position and the financial situation of other economic agents. Hence, the lack of consideration given to balanced economic growth, which meant their analyses, had serious shortcomings. They are two different things to appreciate, one is that public finances' situation often relies on the growth rate, particularly to close the gap with potential growth, and second to check whether the growth assumptions are sustainable in order to measure risks implicit in the budget assumptions.

In this regard, if we neglect the question of growth's sustainability, any analysis of public finances' structural situation, even though it would be supported on a strict comparison between actual and potential growth incurs the risk of being wrong. Yet, the second part of a relevant examination of public finances' situation in the world - the examination of economic growth that provides the context - has been sadly neglected.

iii. Proposals for further macroeconomic surveillance

Economic policy coordination is necessitated by the effects on national macroeconomic imbalances partners. Two situations where they are particularly problematic:

- Inflationary overheating;
- Marked and sustained competitive adjustments episodes that may result in partners' underutilization of capacity.

Also, coordination is particularly necessary in countries deprived of using monetary policy or exchange rate policy to correct imbalances. In addition, financial integration can promote unsustainable economic behavior while international specialization within each zone may increase the risk of asymmetric shocks.

In total, coordination should prevent economic policy implementation made by deferring adjustments to the neighbors or that may hamper the common policies or, more broadly, undermining the market opening. It will enhance global macroeconomic policies' coordination by using peer pressure in these simplified procedures, encouraging moreover national debates evolving in the following directions:

- Deepening global understanding of the basic economic issues and the effect of policies on them;
- Developing diagnostic tools and indicators to assess overall economic conditions;
- Designing international economic policies;
- Establishing a framework for monitoring policies involving high level information exchanges at international level.

Codes of conduct should be internationally adopted to implement fiscal discipline, by intervening on every important issue of economic policy.

On this basis, the case for strengthening monitoring of countries' competitiveness situations and of macro-financial risks (credit, assets, financial capital movements ...) becomes inevitable. Consensus on an operational approach to these variables (competitiveness and financial trends) should be achieved to create guidelines and supervision of their implementation. In this sense, several indicators should be developed, covering:

- real exchange rates;
- labor costs;
- financial markets, credit, assets ...

- with standards for each indicator in order to assess situations and develop information about policies affecting competitiveness, especially in tax matters.

CHAPTER 5

The Crisis' Immediate Effects

The sharp slowdown in economic growth marking the beginning of financial crisis' transmission to the real economy has started to change this view. As this process has accelerated variations have emerged between countries depending on their national budgetary policies orientations.

A. Economic downturn effects: heavier public deficits

Some countries experienced a deceleration of about 1.6 percentage point of GDP. In 2008, countries' nominal deficit increased on average, but on a smaller scale than elsewhere: the growth of fiscal deficits varied, reflecting the uneven crisis impact and the diversity of fiscal impulses. In general, the countries that experienced the greatest slowdown recorded the highest decline in their public balance. However, it is not this economic activity degradation alone that explains public deficits increase. In addition to the impact of automatic stabilizers was added the effect of the fiscal measures adopted, in a piecemeal, by different countries, which led to variations in the damage to the structural balances.

B. Deepening budgetary imbalances

I. The recession and recovery

The crisis' second year was marked by recession, so that GDP continued to shrink despite economic policies' support. Private consumption also showed a decline and the impact was magnified by reduced investments while foreign trade contributed little to growth. One year ago, a very modest recovery occurred. Public support faltered but private consumption became positive again while investment fell much less, and foreign trade contributed positively to the activity.

II. Public deficits' increase and public debt surge

The public balance degradation phenomenon that remained localized to crisis' first year has greatly increased and this process was shared in the world. However, the increase in public accounts deficits' is variable and for some countries, by the relatively small size of their fiscal stimulus programs. This finding may seem more apparent than real because - beyond the support plans - the fall in tax revenues, dramatic for some of them, may be read as a more "spontaneous" public support.

While some countries experienced a serious accumulated deterioration of their public balances, in most countries this decline was slightly lower. Alone, among the top countries, Canada had a relatively limited degradation of these budgetary performances. In most other countries, the cyclical component explains much of the deficit widening. It shows the effect of automatic stabilizers. The automatic stabilizers action appears to be relatively mixed because of economic slowdown's unequal size, which affects different growth deficits relative to potential growth and, public balances' greater or lesser sensitivity based on public interventions level.

But for countries where deficit inflation was particularly strong, the magnitude of fiscal stimulus generally made a difference. It is worth mentioning that the fiscal impulses were divided into roughly equivalent public expenditures acceleration and tax burden reduction. However, some countries based their support on households when other more favored companies. However, at this point, one must complete data on recovery plans alone by automatic stabilizers effect to really appreciate the support given to different agents. In this respect, tax revenues' decline would call particular attention, including for measuring what it owes to unusual collecting facilities and how they were applied to different taxpayers' categories.

Regarding some countries, the bulk of government balance deterioration does not come from the fiscal stimulus but from economic contraction. This component should include budgetary measures taken outside the stimulus and the impact of tax revenues' "normalization", in this case their decrease, corresponding to a return to unit elasticity between tax income and gross domestic product variation (GDP). This means that increasing the deficit (by - 4.9 percentage points of GDP) would come for 3.6 points of GDP from automatic stabilizers. Let's note that automatic stabilizers continue to exercise their countercyclical effect, but in an attenuated manner (+ 0.8 point deficit through public expenditures). But their impact on the balance would be reduced by fiscal impulse shrinkage. Discretionary fiscal policy is restrictive. We move from an expansionary impulse of 1.7 percentage point of GDP to a negative pulse of about 0.3 to 0.5 of GDP on average this year.

III. Crisis economic policies recovery strategies

The fiscal impulse, i.e. discretionary fiscal policy (as opposed to automatic stabilizers) averages 1.1 points of GDP in developed countries, playing a minor part in increasing any public deficit. The outlook for 2011 shows that the impact of countercyclical fiscal policy was concentrated in 2010. Recovery plans are faltering and they represent no more than 0.7 percent of GDP while government deficits remain as high as before. In other words, the structural component of public finance deficit now needs to be reduced.

This situation also shows that G7 countries have undertaken fiscal policies that, even if they all go in the same direction of a countercyclical action, were variable in magnitude. With some reservations regarding the difficulty to establish technically sound diagnoses, it is in United States that the fiscal impulse was strongest. If, on the whole, Western countries have adopted a restrictive fiscal policy, China took a different approach. The already quite uncoordinated fiscal policies of the various states took quite contradictory directions.

The loss of impetus of the measures taken to stem the crisis will have negative consequences for growth, which means there is a need to revisit the monetary and fiscal strategies so far adopted. It must be said that non-conventional monetary policies have led to a significant liquidity surplus, to ensure financial institutions' stability. The surplus will, however, have to be eliminated, to consolidate the crisis and prevent a liquidity excess from feeding a new financial bubble. This withdrawal of funds from central banks will have to be sufficiently ordered and credible in terms of its pace and terms, not to be misinterpreted by economic agents. This involves defining a framework and principles to guide central banks' action, with a phased implementation.

Moreover, this strategic issue is also related to the various fiscal policies adopted to limit the unavoidable impact of fiscal consolidation on economic activity. This particular issue should take into account stability and growth standards involving a coordinated fiscal consolidation from a gradual withdrawal of incentives and structural and fiscal consolidation measures.

The credibility of these strategies taken during the crisis will depend both of the measures taken by governments to limit the risk of the causes of the crisis reoccurring. These measures should aim to correct imbalances in the global economy, which may otherwise persist. The establishment of an enhanced global financial regulation framework is only one aspect of this issue, which requires, above all, a definition of the common possible framework of balanced economic growth regimes.

The nuclear sector in some emerging countries occupies a leading position. However, these states should actively be preparing for the transition to new generation power stations especially with the recent nuclear accident in Japan. There is also substantial variance between countries with certain countries being four or five years in advance of others. Environmental concerns are expected to support the development of this sector despite the current concerns. Several other sectors that are booming include chemicals and pharmaceuticals, biotechnology, environment, including the water industry, food and weapons.

PART THREE

Medium and Long Term Prospects

The potential growth of an economy, reflecting structural changes in the supply factors of capital and labor, now needs to be subject to extra care from economic decision-makers. In this regard, the current crisis will have a negative, deep and lasting impact on potential growth. Such an observation is likely to imply that alarming decisions need to be made about public debt sustainability, precipitating a vigorous public and private growth in saving and stifling a still very hesitant recovery in the bud.

In the context where economic policies are designed primarily to maximize growth, if they were based on an underestimated potential growth, this might prove self-fulfilling. By this is understood the situation where economic policies alone, based on overly pessimistic forecasts, trigger, by their restrictive effects on growth, the occurrence of feared forecasts. Reverse policies do not have the same irreversibility: potential growth measures being particularly imprecise, it is prudent to avoid any policy likely to have irreversible effects.

In addition, the decision made on the potential growth direction, however founded, does not necessarily have to be the right prescription. An examination of the current crisis' root causes calls for the critical issue of growth pattern and ways to ensure sustainability to be re-examined. In particular, in order not to maintain a breeding ground for the emergence of successive crises, which would be detrimental to long term growth and particularly destabilizing for public finances. Also, one of the most obvious current crisis' consequences is, in fact, an unprecedented increase in government debt. Fiscal imbalances' widening is not the result of a spontaneous actions, instead the increase of the debt burden in the GDP results from those countries' interventions in the dual context of their role as insurer of microeconomic risks taken by private agents and their macroeconomic stabilization function in the context of GDP shrinkage.

In sum, reactions to various crisis aspects have increased the numerator of the public debt to GDP ratio while the denominator diminished due to the economic activity's shrinkage is causing a strong increase in public debt burden. This trajectory taken by the public debt during the crisis is obviously unsustainable but it is the result of exceptional circumstances. The fact remains that the public debt sustainability issue is now tackled in terms of the design of a credible debt reduction scenario.

Thus said, the arbitrage conditions between growth and debt reduction are illustrated by five alternative scenarios. What is needed is integration with other economic policies and a higher degree of international coordination to facilitate the orderly reduction in public debts. This renewed international environment could form the beginning of a more tangible control of international balances necessary to prevent future crises.

While recounting the significance of crisis effects on public debts, we note in passing that the gross debt, still significantly higher than the net debt, and a portion of new loans having been devoted to taking stakes in private companies to protect them from bankruptcy. Gross debt is therefore, the only factor considered for stability and growth, in effect it is the only government liabilities. Net debt deducts from this liability the assets funded by loans.

CHAPTER 6

Potential Growth and Prospects for Long-Term Activity

Potential growth can be defined as that producing the maximum production level without accelerating inflation, given the available capacity and manpower. In the current context of marked reduction of economic activity, this has become particularly sensitive and subject to interpretation. Yet it remains a central tool for fiscal and monetary governance.

Potential - or long term - growth is also a key measure for the economic forecast in designing long-term growth scenarios for each country. Neither redoubled doubts as to its extent, nor the attention paid by economic policymakers to this control and surveillance instrument should lead us to forget that potential growth is, in the very long term, essentially determined by innovation rather than budgetary and monetary issues.

A. A structural remedy that involves the long-term

Structurally, actual economic growth "stems" from potential growth, so that this concept is a central element of both economic forecasting and economic governance, which mainly aims, among others, to support the activity. Studying trends is crucial in the face of uncertainty not only about the nature about the expected recovery's sustainability, but also about States' ability to organize their fiscal consolidation in context of structural deficits being closely monitored by the fiscal and market authorities.

I. From potential growth to effective growth

1. Supply factors' primacy in long-term growth

From a short / medium term outlook, economic growth depends mainly on demand factors that are, for example, the international environment for foreign demand, fiscal policy for public demand, wealth distribution facilities and pay evolution for household consumption or business demand.

But from a structural perspective, sometimes known as "long term" supply factors that are:

- The available workforce
- And this workforce's productivity, related to capital intensity and technical progress,
- appear to be determinant.

If we consider these supply factors' evolution, it is possible to estimate, by "addition", the maximum growth that the economy can achieve without strain on production capacity. Any higher growth would lead to an acceleration of inflation. The maximum growth is called "potential growth". In the short term, the effective growth oscillates around the potential growth to the benefit of business cycles. From this perspective, potential growth represents, somehow, cyclical effects' adjusted effective growth. Potential growth becomes tangible over the medium / long term: ideally, effective growth tends on average to converge to this trend.

Effective growth, however, may be permanently lower than potential growth if the economic policy continuously influences growth, to meet a fiscal consolidation constraint. Conversely, effective growth may in a lasting manner exceed potential growth in the event of a dynamic demand to the extent of generating inflation, which is not offset by sufficiently restrictive economic policies or by loss of competitiveness. Of course, from a short-medium term perspective, the growth rate may be higher than the potential growth rate without creating imbalances if there is an initial production deficit.

Note that the potential growth rate is the growth rate of potential output. Potential output is defined as the maximum production yield sustainable in the long term without excessive tension in the economy, and specifically without accelerating inflation. The output gap is the difference between actual output and the potential output level. In short, potential growth is both:

1. An economic analysis tool, useful to fiscal and monetary governance: the potential output level being designed as a supply indicator, the output gap represents the demand excess (or deficiency) and allows an assessment of the situation in the economic cycle;
2. An instrument to generate economic forecasts in the medium and long term, beyond the economic cycle's vicissitudes, and structural recommendations to improve these prospects, for example in terms of activity rates of the labor force or of research and development.

2. *Potential growth determinants*

The growth of production potential of an economy can use only two channels:

- Increasing the available workforce
- And increasing labor productivity.

The increase in wealth per capita is thus essentially permitted by productivity gains. In turn, three factors are likely to contribute to the increase in labor productivity:

- Work hours;
- Capital intensity;
- Total factor productivity.

TFP represents the production increase that cannot be explained by the quantitative evolution of the two apparent production factors that are capital and labor. It should be noted that capital intensity and TFP determine the hourly labor productivity which, combined with work hours, determines the labor productivity. TFP, sometimes described as "unexplained residual" or "Solow residual", can only be explained by the "technical progress" broadly, whose determinants are mainly organizational innovation and progress.

3. *The fundamental role of innovation*

What are the levers to increase the potential growth of an economy, and particularly the global economy's? Greater mobilization of the working age population would raise the level of countries' potential GDP, but this impact can only be transitory. Indeed, the employment rate cannot increase indefinitely, as well as work hours. Specifically, the increase of the workforce today hangs on the evolution of potential growth, despite the structural reforms which tend, *inter alia*, to longer activity duration: is generally distinguished product innovation from process innovation, the latter relating to the production or distribution mode.

In another approach, of integrating organizational progresses, it is possible to identify four types of innovation: product innovation, process innovation (in the strict sense), marketing innovation and organizational innovation.

The "employment rate" is the proportion of employed persons among those of working age (15 years to 64 years). The employment rate reflects an economy's ability to utilize its manpower. It is important to distinguish the magnitude of the rate, which relates the "active population", consisting in the employed and unemployed population, that is to say individuals within the workforce, to the working age population. These two quantities, however, create relations whose meaning is at the heart of labor market policies issues.

Moreover, it appears that a mere accumulation of capital, based on imitation and without the help of innovation, cannot sustain long-term growth for less technologically advanced countries catching up. Generally, without innovation, long-term growth is hampered by the law of production factors' diminishing returns, capital or labor.

In total, "global growth levers", in the long term, the mainspring of growth of GDP per capita, i.e. the mean economic living standard is productivity growth of production factors (capital and labor) via technological progress and innovation. In other words, TFP growth. A sustained investment is essential to prepare for tomorrow's growth, in terms of both production capacity and productivity gains in the strategic context of a "knowledge economy". Investment in research and development would allow a country to sustainably achieve the "growth point" (the one that would bring our medium-term growth to 3% instead of 2%), to reconcile unemployment increases to changes in the public debt and external deficit.

An acceleration of investment, particularly in research and development, sets the conditions for any sustained recovery in productivity, therefore in potential growth and, ultimately, in effective growth. The law of diminishing returns can be formulated as follows: when the firm increases a production factor, capital or labor, while keeping the other fixed, the marginal production necessarily decreases from a certain threshold. The calculation of potential output is based on statistical assumptions and theoretical foundations that do not lead to conclusive results, especially in the context of the current sharp activity slowdown. Estimating potential growth, however, carries important consequences in terms of economic governance.

a. An uncertain measure...

Potential growth's calculation, which can take several approaches, is generally based on a relatively crude model, which involves many assumptions. Today, assessment methods most often mobilize a production function to identify the potential growth determinants' respective contributions. Potential output is usually calculated from a Cobb-Douglas production function, which, with a simple operation, has properties facilitating economic data extraction.

In the potential growth approach, we are essentially interested in the variation of the potential workforce (N^*), of capital stock (K^*) and TFP (A^*). Given the relative inertia of production factors that are capital and labor, TFP's evolution is highly cyclical. Therefore it must be "smoothed" in order to identify, beyond the cycle, the underlying trend. To do this, we generally use the Hodrick-Prescott "filter".

Previously, most countries had used a purely statistical method based on a Hodrick-Prescott filter to estimate the economy position in the cycle. This method appears more suitable for "short term" potential growth's calculation, taking into account the capital accumulation rate that is not consistent with its long-term trend.

Labor and capital: should the series be "smoothed"?

The Hodrick-Prescott filter is generally used for labor input in order to "smooth" the turnover in the number of worked hours. However, most countries consider the actual data, rather than smoothed data on the capital injection. Unlike labor contribution, capital contribution does not need to be corrected in the economy to reach a potential level - the unadjusted capital contribution is already its potential contribution to production. Although the use of capital stock varies significantly over the cycle, the potential capital services flow will always be linked to the total capital stock, not to the amount used at the time.

In the current severe crisis context, the smoothed capital stock measures should generally be filtered by a combination of past and expected values to reduce end of period problems. Therefore, smoothing might add further uncertainty to the current and recent potential output measures. The methods adopted for quantification of these variables may differ depending on the time horizon.

In the short term, potential output is limited by either the productive capital stock, or by the available manpower. It is then necessary to estimate as precisely as possible the maximum utilization degree of each factor not inducing inflationary pressures: production capacity's "normal" utilization rate for capital factor and structural unemployment rate for labor factor that is usually mobilized to assess the labor input contribution to potential production, for example, by subtracting the corresponding number of unemployed persons from active population.

This NAIRU (Non Accelerating Inflation Rate of Unemployment) is the unemployment rate that avoids accelerating inflation, i.e. the rate consistent with stable inflation. When unemployment falls below the NAIRU, the number of jobseekers decreases, nominal wage increases as well as workers' bargaining power. However, companies increase their prices to face their own increases in expenditure then inflation increases. However, when the unemployment rate is higher than the NAIRU, workers' bargaining power weakens to the extent that firms can lower their costs and prices: in effect, inflation decreases.

The NAIRU is finally equal to the unemployment rate for which inflation remains constant. Phillips curve expresses the inverse relationship between unemployment and inflation. The different levels of the NAIRU observed in space and time are often presented as the consequence of structural differences in, notably, labor markets, for example in terms of rules, activity behaviors or workforce structures by age and gender. Therefore, "structural policies", aimed at improving potential growth, often planned labor market reforms in the objective, inter alia, to lower the NAIRU. In the neo-liberal theoretical framework, the NAIRU is based on imperfect competition in goods and labor markets that gives employers the power to set prices above marginal cost, and employees, the power to require a higher real wage rate at the labor marginal productivity level.

Therefore, a significant reduction in the NAIRU can be obtained by implementing a policy to increase competition in the goods market (between incumbents and potentially entrants firms) and the labor market (between primary and secondary segments, but also between "insiders" - those who have a job, and "outsiders" - those who do not). Highlighted in 1958, the Phillips curve empirically illustrates an inverse relationship, between unemployment and the growth of nominal wages. The "communicating vessels" phenomenon between unemployment and inflation has been marked by crisis in the seventies, with a concomitant increase in unemployment and inflation in the medium term, implying a rising NAIRU.

The NAIRU concept can be distinguished from the, anterior, one of natural unemployment rate, although they are often confused. This concept, put forward by Milton Friedman, represents an equilibrium unemployment rate to which the economy tends in long term. But the more one thinks long term, the more potential growth determinants can be reduced to two fundamental variables, which derive from the previous ones: the labor force and technical progress. When the perspective moves into the future, we can indeed consider that capital adjusts to the economy needs and that structural unemployment revolves around a certain equilibrium value.

It appears that the potential output approach - and therefore potential growth - has both elements of:

- Uncertainty when it comes to determining the potential growth horizon and useful variables
- And fragility:
    - in terms of method, especially due to the fact that technical progress rate changes are particularly difficult to explain and therefore to anticipate, making any forecasting exercise relatively perilous,
    - and in relation to data collection, availability of labor and capital are not directly observable, for example, estimating the structural unemployment rate usually involves expert judgment.

With the crisis, potential output estimates have, in general, been revised. Relevant studies generally specify that the current circumstances make it particularly difficult to assess economies' supply potential, so that the error margins are larger than usual. Thus, it will take time and analyses to reassess the potential output and those initial estimates should be regarded only as a first result. The theory of natural unemployment rate implies that the whole equilibrium unemployment is voluntary; while the NAIRU incorporates labor market imperfections (information asymmetries, friction, etc...) and does not exclude the existence of involuntary equilibrium unemployment. The concept of natural unemployment has been questioned since the eighties, which saw the clearly unintentional emergence of mass unemployment. This perspective is consistent with the neoclassical Solow growth model.

Sensitivity of the output gap estimates at the end of period treatment

A recurring problem with estimating the potential output and the output gap is the "problem of closure", which arises because most methods, even those based on a production function framework, filter out at least a part of data sets to identify the underlying trend. The problem of closure arises because if a series' last historical value corresponds to a cyclical peak or, conversely, to a cyclical trough, the corresponding filtered series can give a misleading view of the underlying predicted trend. The approach commonly adopted to overcome this difficulty is to apply the filter to retrospective series completed by projected values.

From another perspective, a more fundamental criticism is emerging: the production function based on the capital and labor mobilization does not include natural resources as a primary factor. However, as potential growth stumbles on the speed of capital accumulation and the increase in the labor force, it now seems clear that limited natural resources may be in the long term an additional ceiling to growth missed by previous arguments.

b. ... but a real influence on economic governance

Potential output and growth measures can have serious consequences. For example, when production slows, expansionary economic policies are appropriate if the slowdown comes from a lack of demand in terms of production capacity; they then allow a return towards full employment with a return to growth which usually leads to a large "flow" of these policies.

However, these policies should normally avoided if it is potential growth itself that is the constraint, as they are then likely to cause some adverse effects, which are mainly, alternatively or cumulatively, inflation, trade balance deterioration and a sustainable public debt increase since the effective growth does not increase enough to offset the increased deficit effects on the public debt burden in GDP.

Potential growth and economic policies: dangerous liaisons?

False estimates may have serious consequences on economic policies' relevance and some believe that, in the past, fundamental governance errors have been made due to erroneous potential growth estimates.

According to some analyses, potential growth was significantly overvalued on several occasions, such as when economies underwent a sustained growth period in the years after 2000, leading some to delay necessary fiscal consolidation as the strong growth prospects made that appear less relevant. On the other hand, during the seventies' and eighties' recessions, they had followed policies that were too favorable to demand expansion and this had resulted in inflation acceleration.

According to others, it was regularly underestimated - if not exploited - since the early nineties to justify restrictive monetary policies that would have, in excess, influenced growth. From diagnosis to treatment, conceptual preferences are not indifferent; in reality, the more an economist is "Keynesian" ("monetarist"), the more he/she tends to consider the "output gap" as high (low).

The topic is not only partly subjective, but it appears, in another hand, relatively constrained. Potential output has certainly been affected by the crisis, but estimating an order of magnitude is difficult ... and dangerous. In fact, two types of problems could occur when a substantial drop in potential GDP is reported.
First, such a message could lead central bankers to raise their interest rates to fight against any inflation risk, thereby endangering the end of crisis.

Secondly, governments would be more likely to precipitate a fiscal austerity policy, again at the risk of curbing a fledgling recovery, as assumptions of lower potential growth will feed into higher assumptions about the structural deficit. Finally, we must reckon with the partially self-fulfilling nature of the announcements made regarding potential growth: potential growth differentials between countries are likely to guide investment, and in turn influence both growth and jobs.

CHAPTER 7

The Instrument of a Regained Ambition

In a "Schumpeterian" perspective, it is possible that the occurrence of an innovation wave is partly responsible for the end of the current economic crisis, with new productions that replace or add to old ones. Moreover, sustainable development requires new industries or production methods and new approaches to welfare.

Research is a crucial activity for humanity's future is vital for recovery across many sectors. Health, environment, physical and food security, energy are global public properties and it is clear that research alone will provide for the long term. Dare we say, research is itself a global public property.

Insofar as research and innovation could also condition, for the future, new productions are likely to help the world out of the economic and environmental rut in which it seems to sink today, the "global public property" qualification is of singular relevance. In Schumpeter's approach, depression is a period of questioning of now oversized productive structures, debt reduction and the gestation of new innovations. Each cycle's duration depends on the speed and effect of innovation.

In the current economic climate, we must insist that the quest for accounts balance in the medium term not to lead to burdening the research capacity, both public (budgetary expenditure) and private (via fiscal and social expenditures), without prejudice, of course, with the necessary evaluation of these expenditures' efficiency to move towards an optimal resources allocation.

Nor should it lead to ignoring the development of investment, without which the future would be sacrificed to the present and future generations left with an unlivable legacy. So here it is essential that the global fiscal governance, should guide its strategy not only in short and medium term but also in medium and long term. Therefore, the "great debt" allocations to encourage research and innovation expenditures would fit *a priori* in countries' orientations, and articulate with both research and budgetary policies.

With the benefit of an extensive international coordination, it is possible that the implementation of actions financed by debt should be guided by the desire to entrench a substantial portion of its profits in the countries without "exporting" more than is sensible the additional actual (demand driven) or potential (supply-driven) growth that it will cause.

A. Potential growth forecasts and scenarios

The labor and capital constraints will influence the medium-long term on potential growth evolution in most major industrialized countries but the orientation of the TFP contribution is more uncertain. The question of how the current global crisis will impact potential growth is much more debated. Estimates call for a few caveats. In most cases, the global crisis is analyzed as a demand shock that has pushed effective growth below potential growth level and widening the initial output gap. Thus, as a first approach, what characterizes the recent economic situation is the increasing gap between the effective demand level and the available supply level and not a potential growth drop. This reading of the crisis is supported by the evolution of aggregate demand, with a break from their long-term trends, and supply indicators (such as rising unemployment and falling production capacity utilization rates). It justifies the intervention of Keynesian countercyclical policies to revive the effective demand. Thus, *prima facie*, the crisis is not a potential output crisis.

However, the question of this demand crisis' structural impact over potential supply arises (at least as it is raised by large economic institutions and many economists), and from this occurs the question of the crisis effects on potential growth in the medium to long term. From the outset it should be noted that with this issue, we recognize explicitly that an output gap resulting from a bout of weakness in demand may turn into a prolonged potential growth crisis, that is to say supply. In other words, the question of potential growth is not only a supply structural problem but also a demand adjustment matter and Keynesian policies can be seen as contributing to the preservation of the economy's potential growth.

It was also one of their explicit justifications. This was a major challenge for crisis policies to reconcile as quickly as possible actual production and potential output. To that must be added a goal to identify the links between demand support policies and the preservation, and even increase, of the supply capacity. The latter was reflected differently according to the support plans: by raising both the priority given to investment support and partial unemployment benefits measures.

Which mechanisms would favor the demand crisis effects on economies' potential growth?

Two transmission channels are mainly identified:

- Braking of capital accumulation;
- The scarcity of labor.

These two channels are ambiguous. With the existence of spare production capacity may be associated subtle effects on potential growth. On the one hand, the availability of an unsaturated production apparatus offers margins to production revival that allows the utilization of a high effective growth potential. In other words, it demonstrates a continued growth potential despite the fall in effective demand. On the other hand, it weighs on the effective growth potential (first, why invest if excess capacity exists; then the falling capital profitability should weigh on investment) and long term potential growth (maintenance of an investment is less efficient than new investments that would have occurred without the crisis). Similarly, rising unemployment may more or less imply downward revisions of potential growth depending on whether it results or not in a permanent exclusion (and thus definite for part of the workforce, the most elderly in particular) from the labor market. In this regard, partial unemployment incentives seem to have benefited from a happy inspiration.

In sum, much will depend on the crisis' length. The earlier the revival will occur, the lower the growth potential will have been undermined. This argument supports those who advocate continuation of economic policies aiming at a strong and fast recovery. For long-term projections, made on the basis of a "creeping" evolution of the workforce, TFP's contribution is crucial. But any unequivocal TFP progression forecast is based on fragile conjectures, hence the relevance of the scenarios, which allow considering several potential growth trajectories. However, we must go beyond and question the establishment of more sustainable growth patterns.

In the potential growth estimates, some factors - those related to quantitative increase in output - are almost physical factors while others result from a calculation whose results reflect a given economic equilibrium state. This is particularly the case for capital accumulation - which depends on historical profitability levels that are contingent - and productivity gains - which, partly contingent too, are amenable to a similar judgment. One lesson of the current global crisis may have to be that the return on capital was based on unsustainable financial factors. Thus, productivity losses could have benefited from more apparent than real gains.

If this suspicion is proved true, and if imbalances of recent past growth patterns should not continue, it would necessary to either revise downwards potential growth prospects or rely on different growth patterns.

I. *The probably negative crisis impact on labor productivity in the short to medium term*

Two main reasons are advanced: the fall in firms' and households' investment expenditures and an increase in structural unemployment. The loss of dynamism is mainly driven by the sharp downturn in the capital stock and rising structural unemployment. These two effects, acting negatively in a recession, are by nature temporary and will reverse in the recovery phase. Countries' reforms will support potential growth recovery. Thus, enterprises' economic efficiency and competitiveness will be stimulated by business tax reduction and structural reforms (training, establishment of employment center, law of employment reasonable offer, law of economy modernization, and creation of the labor income) contribute to increased participation rates and lower structural unemployment, while bolstering productivity. Other potential growth determinants would not be affected by the crisis. One can reasonably assume that the outlook for factors' total productivity remains unchanged. Indeed, the crisis impact on the overall productivity is ambiguous: the disappearance of the least efficient production units would increase the structural productivity. In total, it is assumed that TFP would maintain its pre-crisis growth rate linked in particular with the expected effects of economic modernization and research tax credits' successive reforms.

The labor and capital factors are involved, for most countries, in a marked change in potential growth:

These elements are not exclusive to an ulterior recovery, and, in any event, do not engage the future global potential growth trajectory. Anyway, it seems that the crucial factor may suffer from a long term higher risk aversion while the NAIRU, whose inertia is strong, would be likely to suffer from rising unemployment, TFP orienting *a priori* in a more uncertain manner.

1. *The capital factor adversely affected by higher risk aversion?*

A sustained increase in the cost of capital results in a lower equilibrium output level. The investment collapse and the related slowdown in the growth of capital input to production will contribute two-thirds to the expected decline in potential growth in the short term. We cannot exclude that the decreases in capital intensity may persist in the medium term due to a sustained cost of capital inflation, linked to higher risk aversion, which would take a structural nature.

At the very least, financial institutions' and the markets' propensity to take risks in order to finance investment could reach its medium term level, given that the period before the financial crisis was characterized by a certain euphoria. The distribution of capital contributions to the decline in potential growth shows a proportionally greater contribution of Anglo-Saxons, indeed marked by more tangible credit shrinkage. Moreover, the crisis is notoriously conducive to a sustained decline in labor input and participation rates (workforce).

2. *The possibility of a hysteresis effect for labor input*

The structural unemployment rate, defined as the unemployment rate consistent with stable inflation, is usually regarded as stable, over the longer term. However, the particular deep crisis context, accompanied by a sharp and probably lasting increase in unemployment, requires assumptions about decisive changes in the structural unemployment rate in the short and medium term. It will expect an adverse effect with two main possible explanations:

- Reduced "outsiders'" bargaining power (that is to say those excluded from the labor market, often in long duration unemployment situations), who cannot make, alongside the insiders, any salary requirements, and help to balance supply and demand in the labor market;
- Relatively rapid human capital obsolescence when unemployment duration is prolonged, especially for certain skills; it may lead to, for a certain portion of the population, long-term unemployment, even when the employment prospects improves. It seems that the incidence of long-term unemployment does increase as unemployment rises, which supports the hypothesis of an adverse effect, although international organization's recommendations about economic policy usually tend to lower it.

Hysteresis is the property of a system that tends to remain in an altered state when ceased the external cause that produced the change of state. This is known as unemployment hysteresis if he does not imply a return to the initial unemployment rate when ceases the cause (economic crisis) of its increase.

The distribution of work contributions to lower potential growth reflects the traditional opposition of United States, characterized by low unemployment hysteresis effects, and other countries, where this effect would be greater because of the more stigmatizing character that has, in general, employment loss. Employment's proportionately large contribution for specific countries can be explained by the forecast, for the latter, of a comparatively high TFP contribution. Related to capital contribution, labor contribution to a lower potential output of these countries will no longer appear off-centered compared with other developed countries.

In terms of actual unemployment rate, it will only recede gradually. Meanwhile, the unemployment rate would increase 5 points in United States. Constructing an economic policy based on estimates represents a certain danger: that of seeing uncertain expectations come true, self-fulfilling expectations phenomenon that should be avoided. Rapid crisis unwinding is a condition of avoiding phenomena described herein that are not only hypothetical but are by no means inevitable.

The risk taken by economic policies based on downward potential growth revisions, which would be excessive, is much greater today than that of policies taking by the opposite extreme, if only because these two policies are not equally reversible.

3. *Opposed risks for total factor productivity?*

If the crisis effects on TFP are potentially important, they are difficult to quantify, especially since they support both an improvement and a decrease in total productivity. The crisis leads to the abandonment of the least productive activities, which goes in the direction of improving productivity. However, the prospect of a lower financial activities contribution, particularly intense before the crisis, to national wealth, and especially in the longer term, reductions in research and development expenditure, are consistent with lessening TFP. From this angle, United Kingdom and United States appear relatively more sensitive. In respect of these two countries, the problem mentioned above of setting up of a more sustainable growth pattern can be explored in detail.

In total, there is rather a pro-cyclical effect of crises on R&D, mainly due to credit constraints; the decline in firms' R&D is particularly high, when profits are falling, since they are dependent on financial markets. The crisis, marked by the credit crunch, is likely to cause a decline in innovation expenditure by challenging the most promising investments in the long term. Each recessive shock would cost more than its initial impact because long-term projects are amputated at the cycle bottom, for reasons of funds but also labor availability. Less time and money are devoted to basic research but also to the development stage, disabling the subsequent recovery.

If innovative projects are the guarantee of productivity increases causing expansion periods, the current crisis' depth is, conversely, likely to cause a hysteresis effect, requiring public expenditures' adjustments. However, countries themselves, subject to increasing budgetary constraints, could be encouraged, starting next year, to reduce credit or tax expenditure on research support. Nevertheless, countries retain a near stabilization of TFP contribution to growth potential, which may be considered to indicate optimism, despite the political will displayed in today's R&D.

CHAPTER 8

The Expected Slowdown in Workforce

In the short and medium term, the activity rate may decline because of difficulties on the labor market and the increased use of early retirement. Conversely, in countries where pensions are mainly funded, losses on pension assets due to lower stock prices may encourage, if not force, some workers to delay their retirement. Migration flows' reaction to economic slowdown is another uncertainty for all industrialized countries.

The G7 was characterized by a relative dynamism, with a labor contribution to potential growth covering contrasting realities: a significant demographic advantage, but a setback in activity level. It remains that in the longer term, a significant reversal of workforce increase, consistent with global population ageing, even if relative, seems inevitable. This development corresponds to an almost zero workforce annual contribution to potential growth throughout the period. It should however be recalled that at one time, these projections were good news for breaking with the previous prospect of a significant workforce decrease. In addition to more favorable scenarios regarding the dependency ratio's long-term evolution, projections on potential growth have therefore been revised upwards. Finally, we observe that if the workforce's loss of impetus greatly affects structural growth, it leads to a shift in unemployment short-term changes, which is less negative than it would have been if the workforce had risen at the earlier rate.

In the context of a sharp deterioration in the labor market, the employment policy, through the social treatment, will not play its stabilizing role in unemployment. After amplifying rising unemployment, new jobs in the non-profit sector will just return to the levels observed in early 2008. Workforce's cyclical decline will eventually be the main unemployment damper.

This finding in mitigation should not minimize the magnitude of employment deterioration: the largest decrease over the past 25 years.

A. Between breathlessness and continued growth potential

Looking forward there are five potential scenarios that can be divided into two groups. This choice is deliberate. Given the uncertainties, it is the diversity of possibilities that we must now consider. In one group, the long term potential growth would remain fixed, labor productivity rising slightly each year and no increase for the workforce. In the other, the potential growth would drop. If financial crises' impact on potential output is generally negative, their effect is less pronounced on long term potential growth. What is deliberately not addressed that issue of the effects of the implementation of environmental policies on long-term growth.

From a macroeconomic perspective, there can be no short to medium term "green growth" with current growth measure tools. But the question is different when it is considered over the long term. It is particularly important to measure the macroeconomic cost of environmental inaction.

Anyway, it seems reasonable to develop scenarios based on potential growth set at the same over the next decade. It will be noted in particular that, in the long run, the global economy has successive growth phases, characterized by annual growth rates revolving around different values: these values can be considered, on a preliminary approach, as potential growth values characterizing, with some consistency, each of these phases. Being a logarithmic scale, the slope of the blue curve is always proportional to growth. Relatively homogeneous and durable "phases" then appear (for example, the "thirty glorious years", followed by a period in which the average growth rate substantially bends).

I. The assumption of a continued global potential growth

If potential growth was to continue in the long term, several scenarios would be possible on the shorter term effective output evolution. First, it is conceivable that effective output will eventually reach potential output and the output gap would be absorbed through sustained growth, above trend, despite the significant fiscal consolidation effort.

Two reduction patterns of the output gap are considered, each giving rise to a scenario:

- A gradual reduction, with an effective average annual growth leading to a "closure" of the output gap within 10 years, then effective growth settling around potential growth;
- A rapid absorption, with an effective annual growth within the next 5 years, which declines thereafter, leading to a "closure" of the output gap with effective growth gravitating around potential growth. Full employment will be realized gradually as we approach the closure of the output gap, in favor of a linear unemployment rate decline in the baseline scenario, and in 2015 in the secondary scenario. Then, it is possible that potential growth remains in the

long-term oriented along that trend, but that the potential production loss caused by the crisis does not go away.

Under these conditions, the average effective growth gravitates around the status quo from year to year, so that the output gap will never close. The unemployment rate curve would remain flat throughout the period. That is to say effective output will have reached potential output. Note that a public deficit reduction program should generally be accompanied by other agents' (households and enterprises) reducing their savings to enable the economic circuit's closure in a safeguarded growth context. Average long term growth is here fixed across these three scenarios.

The first two scenarios seem very proactive; reconciling ending the crisis and gradual public finances consolidation, they imply not only a substantial decline in household savings, but a significant investment pick up. All five scenarios are also based on the assumption that trading partners' prices would evolve so as to stabilize global competitiveness, so for example, foreign demand in Canada will remain strong throughout the period. To this should be added that the future output gap closure in the baseline scenario assumes an effective growth averaging 2.5%, this perspective adds to the optimism of this scenario for the early years; if it is considered that due to the amount of programmed public deficit reduction effort, it would be reduced by 5% of GDP within two years to limit public debt's growth. This effort is a potentially negative effect of such a fiscal policy on economic growth. Thus, in this scenario, the global economy should grow spontaneously even if its past behavior shows that this assumption is not feasible, and such vigorous growth would be unusual. Unemployment is on average falling steadily in the baseline scenario, where the effective growth rate only slightly exceeds productivity's. Unemployment falls rapidly in Scenario 2, where the growth rate far exceeds labor productivity's in the context of workforce slower growth: full employment is achieved in 5 years. The decline occurs gradually during the output gap closure.

The third scenario shows, however, that growth alone, all things being roughly equal, cannot stem public debt snowballing into a worse deficit: higher effective growth rate is necessary in the expected (and predictable) fiscal policy conditions. Meanwhile, unemployment is stagnating at a high level, effective growth no greater than labor productivity increased by workforce progression rate.

Each of the three previous scenarios is a stylization of the global economy's possible trajectories, to which it is difficult to assign a probability. However, we can give some insights, particularly on the basis of recent global economic history. It seems that recessions usually resulted in permanent production losses, especially recessions associated with financial crises. Financial crises permanently lower potential output on average. However, the financial crises' effect on potential growth is less certainly negative.

In this perspective, the scenario 3, with a definite production loss coupled with a continued potential growth, seemed plausible, if it was not for the aggravating circumstance of potential growth slowdown linked to a loss of impetus in workforce progression. Fortunately, there are probably substantial productivity gains related to Governments' efficiency. For an unprecedented effort to optimize public expenditure, a significant and sustainable increase in public investment, source of growth and employment, is possible. Under these conditions, maintenance, in the long term, of potential growth (based on labor productivity rising at the steady rate of 1.9% instead of 1.6% before the crisis) does not seem unrealistic. Even if part of the excitement must be attributed to the fact that is not envisaged, in this scenario, a reduction of the growth gap. But without a strong policy supporting productivity (or without a providential technological leap), no marked change in potential growth should be expected.

II. The hypothesis of a potential growth failure

It should be considered a sustainable potential growth inflection, in two ways logical regard to the evolution of demographic conditions and of the current crisis' consequences. Besides the lasting hysteresis effects on TFP, the expenditure decline induced by a long fiscal consolidation could affect the supply factors: production capacity and available workforce. These effects combine then with the decline in the workforce to diminish potential growth. A decline in potential growth would, however, lead to a faster output gap closure, as the result of two scenarios proposed here:

- In the first scenario, the potential growth dips. However, effective growth is set starting next year, as in the baseline scenario. Filling the output gap is much faster than in the first scenario, and output gap closure is reached in 9 years, the year starting which effective growth slows;
- In a second scenario, potential growth dips but, as in the previous scenario, the effective growth was 2.5%. Filling the output gap is

even faster: the output gap closure occurs in 6 years, year after which effective growth slows.

As in scenarios N°1 and N°2, full employment is achieved gradually as is the output gap closure, in favor of a linear unemployment rate. Wages grow more slowly (at the same rate as productivity) and private agents' efforts (low savings rate and rising investment rates), though still substantial, are reduced to less unusual proportions. In addition, productivity gains lower than in Scenario N°1 allow faster return to full employment based on the same effective growth: work being less productive, more assets are needed to achieve a certain production level.

However, this trajectory implies that the evolution of each country's productivity does not decide on its trading partners', because a productivity shift, specific to each country, could lead to loss of competitiveness that could greatly affect employment, in the long term, even if wage gains were adjusted. In this case, indeed, the virtuous coordination resulting from strong growth in terms of capital accumulation is more hypothetical. The public debt' trajectory tends, however, to grow, especially in Scenario N° 5, prepared on the basis of a limited long term potential growth.

Apart from their effects on economic policies' design, both scenarios have the advantage of illustrating potential growth's impact on the purchasing power prospects. The decrease is roughly linear and is fully achieved at output gap closure. The increase is roughly linear and is fully achieved with output gap closure. A potential GDP shift would have a medium term impact on effective GDP and therefore on GDP per capita, with inevitable consequences on the average evolution of the purchasing power.

Potential growth comes from labor productivity and workforce growth. To derive projections of increased labor productivity, GDP per capita trends, must be taken into account the demographic structure. It is scalable, so that the working age population is not correlated to the number of inhabitants. It is observed that, meanwhile; the workforce should stop its progression, which reflects the anticipation of a downward growth potential shift, even in the case of unchanged labor productivity.

In total, the average annual potential growth per capita should be equal to the potential growth, adjusted by the population's growth rate. In turn, taking into account population's growth cannot account for changes in the number of households, which often represents the basic unit to increase the purchasing power. In fact, the number of households is increasing faster than population and this difference should increase with ageing populations. Under these conditions, with a global average increase in the number of households per year, effective growth would leave no room for gains in purchasing power per household.

Regarding assets' purchasing power, a new issue will be the Western Ageing population. If we consider (in addition to increased levies prospects that may result from a public re-saving movement to reduce the current public debt level), the significant increase in the population more than 70 years old, whose needs in terms of health and dependency, are the most important, transfer income to fund the set formed by pensions, health and dependency, appear set to increase in significant proportions, and workforce's purchasing power to bend, as a result of increased levies.

In sum, productivity support is a major issue, because a higher potential growth would allow following a growth path without too much critical tension on the changes in assets, disposable income and on public finances. A value added distribution more supportive of work remuneration could be usefully developed. Supporting assets income, whose spending would promote investment, which some consider mainly hampered by the historically low production capacity utilization rate, would result in enhanced production potential. But with consumption internationalization, this type of policy can be fully effective only if it is applied by each country's major trading partners.

CHAPTER 9

How Might Public Finances Balance for the Medium and Long Term?

A. The medium-term horizon

The long term public finances prospects are dependent on the public finances projection in the medium term. They describe a gradual return to a public deficit level that stabilizes the influence of public debt on GDP. Fiscal policy is strongly oriented in the direction of reducing the structural deficit in the context of strong economic recovery. This scenario assumes a configuration that can be judged favorable in terms of the economic situation and of more structural sequences.

Essentially, they reflect a tightening of fiscal policy. They do not necessarily address the problems exposed. Some of these changes, still in the forecasts, consist of correcting the very short term prospects: the public deficit of the base year is slightly lower than expected. Accordingly, that year's deficit was revised to -0.5 average GDP percentage points. This difference comes mainly from interest charges which are on average lower by 0.4 GDP percentage point. In these circumstances, public debt will be reduced by one GDP percentage point.

The most significant change relates to the overall fiscal policy. The additional public balance adjustment reached 1.6 GDP percentage point over the next three years or 0.53 GDP percentage point over a year. This does not come from more favorable growth assumptions. The cyclical balance is changing as in our projections. The difference is thus in the structural balance and adds to interest charges reduction. The consecutive structural adjustment would be stronger than previously announced. It is now generally expected to reduce next year's structural deficit. This fiscal policy tightening is not accompanied by a revision of growth prospects. In total, industrialized countries' public debt is at a level lower than 5 GDP percentage points compared to projections.

Thus, with increased fiscal voluntarism and without adverse effects on economic growth, stability programs would enhance the prospect of a gradual decline of public debt's weight on GDP in G7, reducing the likelihood of triggering unpleasant mechanics.

I. Gradual return to a public deficit that stabilizes public debt level in GDP...

Government balances would further deteriorate by 0.4 percentage points on average this year. Beyond that, the public finance program expects an improvement in the public administration financial balance. This sequence corresponds, with a few tenths of point's error margin, to industrialized countries' public finances' multiyear programming. General government deficit would begin to withdraw this year and would be reduced to 5% of the various GDP in two years. The deficit reduction effort made by the various Governments would be particularly large.

In total, a 5 GDP percentage points deficit would remain in 2013 in most countries, of which two thirds (3.3 points) is due to the States, with the remainder almost entirely related to social security for those who have it. However, the deficit level reached at the end of period would not be such that the various public debts' in the GDP is stabilized by this time. It would have to be of the order of 1 GDP percentage point. This represents slightly more than the annual structural deficit reduction effort as planned if the global public debt level is stabilized and begins to recede.

II. ... With tonic growth...

The global public finance program assumes on average an annual tonic growth during the next three years (4.3% in nominal data). This scenario assumes economic growth whose acceleration will gradually erase the output gap accumulated during the crisis. In other words, among the three possible crisis impacts, only the activity pick up, during the program period, will allow a return to the path of long term growth at the cost of a recovery with effective growth rate transiently exceeding potential growth rate.

It may also be noted that this scenario implies a sharp increase in global payroll, which would rise in value by 5% per annum, or more than the GDP. This assumption would increase wages' share in value added, which will be conducive to dynamic tax burden by its effects on consumption, income and wages.

III. ... And fiscal policies structural adjustment

To these economic conditions, which would result in significant improvement in tax revenues and a gradual cyclical deficit makeup, would be added to the fiscal policy choices' effects. This fiscal policy should be oriented towards reducing the structural deficit in the sequence indicating, in addition, changes in government balance's both components: expenditures and revenues.

The tax burden would increase in each country. A portion of the tax revenue, lost during the crisis, will be regained with the return to unitary tax elasticity greater than in the context of a tax bases increase stronger than that resulting from a simple return to potential growth. As for global public expenditures, they will grow less than anticipated growth and potential growth conditioning public expenditure weight decrease in the various GDP and structural improvement of balances.

The latter, strong this year, because the combined effect of changes in tax burden and public expenditures, would thereafter rise by between 0.6 and 0.7 GDP percentage points mainly due to public expenditure dropping out. This is in total due to an average countries contribution of about 2009/10 to public deficit decrease achieved during this period that structural balance will be adjusted, of which 2.5 improvement points in the government balance would come from a structural recovery. The planned effort will be higher but insufficient for intermediate public debt stabilization.

IV. A public debt whose increase slope flattens

Global public debt would rise this year by over 30 GDP percentage points compared to 2007. In particular, increased debt burdens assumed that other costs do not either do not rise further over the next two years, or at a lower than historical rate. Public debt has increased, mainly as a result of refinancing policies implemented following the financial crisis. Subsequent increases come, for their part, from the combination of rising public deficits and deteriorating nominal growth. The overall expected recovery is not strong enough to offset the effect of increasing debt from international public deficits. Measures are taken only because of their effects on gross public debt, in most countries. A more complete review should reflect the assets built up in return for this debt. In addition, global public debt would continue its growth but on a very slow pace due to the combination of continued decrease of the various public deficits and increased growth.

V. An economic configuration conducive to public debt mastering

Besides growth trends, the breakdown in public expenditure, which should be further enhanced if global public debt costs should rise, fiscal adjustment will involve a spontaneous GDP growth significantly stronger than the usual global economy performance. Assuming a multiplier effect of fiscal policies by 1 in the short term, spontaneous economic growth should raise enough to have the effective growth that serves as the public finances underlying. This configuration is not unattainable, the world having already experienced, over the past 30 years, two periods during which economic growth (adjusted fiscal policy) grew at this average rate for three years.

Still, the number of episodes is quite low and the economically painless sustained fiscal adjustment period has been accompanied by changes in the economic environment that contributed to this relative safety. It is emphasized in this context that maintaining an accommodative monetary policy capable of anchoring financial and credit markets' behavior in the direction of interest rates favorable to growth seems to be a key to success of fiscal adjustments. They are also dependent on the international economic environment, increased demand from outside and from countries that have embarked on fiscal adjustment relaying economic growth. The question now is whether these "facilitating rules" will be met or not?

This question is not only for the medium term, but also for the short term, since the global public finances trajectory requires a stronger and faster end to the crisis. On monetary policy, which does not seem able to be more accommodating than now, moreover under penalty of inefficiency elsewhere, monetary conditions could improve with unclear implications. The improvement comes from a "normalization" of the credit eligibility conditions. This event is hampered, however, by private agents' (firms and households) financial position and a reluctance to borrow in a period of great uncertainty regarding the growth potential. Without improvement in expectations, the prospects offered by credit conditions loosening will not have significant effects.

Moreover, assuming that the funding demand is generated again by private agents, the risk exists that, therefore, the conditions imposed on borrowers would rise. In this case, fiscal adjustments undertaken to control the global public debt would become more demanding. We cannot exclude a further escalation of tensions in certain sovereign countries' markets, whose impact on other countries could, in turn, be a source of financial destabilization. Below a certain interest rates level opens a liquidity trap, which reduces the volume of available funds.

On the second point, the difficulties seem even greater. They come from the fact that all leading countries experienced a recession, that is to say, they converged downwards. In addition, about equally everywhere, a deterioration of the public finances occurred. In other words, all these countries must bounce back while facing the same problem of fiscal consolidation.

In such a situation, one may a priori fear that all States simultaneously adopt restrictive policies that would each result in deflation and in an endless race to fiscal adjustment. However, the game theory lessons provide some comfort here. Assuming that all countries share the view that major budgetary adjustments would exert strong depression effects that would "benefit" others only, the theory shows that every country could resist the temptation to do too much. But it is possible that all countries do not adopt this view. The announcements made by some European countries (Netherlands, Germany in particular) suggest a fiscal policy tightening with which France appears to agree, but with a commendable restraint.

B. Public finances to 2030

I. A neutral global fiscal policy face to five economic scenarios

Long term public finances' projection in the world requires fiscal policy assumptions to provide a macroeconomic framework. The choice was made to test what would happen under a neutral global fiscal policy on the global public debt trajectory in the world. Other assumptions would not have the same scope since then the informative results would be themselves entirely in the assumptions. It should be remembered that all fiscal policies considered here would follow a policy, which, in the medium term, would bring the international public balance progressively closer to the level likely to stabilize public debt's weight in GDP.

1. A neutral global fiscal policy

In the scenarios presented here, countries' fiscal policy follows the same guidelines. The changes in public revenue and stability program expenditure over the medium term are not sustained for the long term: moving on to hypotheses corresponding to a neutral fiscal policy in 4 years. For public revenue, we assume that all loss of revenue caused by the crisis will be recovered but then the tax burden will reflect the GDP. Thus the tax burden rate will become stable in accordance with mechanisms triggered by a return to a unitary GDP income elasticity.

For public expenditure (the only primary expenditure), after having progressed with less than potential growth, this will evolve like the latter beyond the next 2 years. Interest expenses were, in turn, on a dependent dynamic to the cost of debt level, linked to developments in the nominal interest rate and its deviation from the growth rate.

2. *Five economic scenarios*

Five scenarios to illustrate the burden of uncertainty regarding the outcome of the current crisis and the long term growth rate on the public finances' trajectory:

- A central scenario of growth above potential until filling the output gap achieved in the long term, followed by growth in parallel with potential growth;
- A scenario of potential and effective growth with a cyclical rebound strong in three years and then reduced;
- A scenario of potential and effective growth but no bounce, so that the deviation from potential output resulting from the crisis is never caught up;
- A scenario of slower potential growth;
- A scenario of a stronger slowdown of potential growth.

In the latter two cases, the slowdown in potential growth allow anticipating the return on the path of potential output whose activity the crisis has disrupted, for the latter case, the worst in terms of potential. However, it is important to note that the potential return does not come from a cyclical recovery but from a mere decrease between effective growth rate and potential growth rate originating from a deceleration of the latter. For public finances, these scenarios correspond to economic contexts more or less favorable to public accounts' recovery. In short, this is basically to test fiscal policy adequacy to different possible macroeconomic developments.

II. *Contrasting public accounts trajectories*

Not surprisingly, changes in government accounts in the various countries involved in these five scenarios are very different. The spread of government deficits have their consequences in the of increased public debt levels.

1. *The evolution of deficit*

Regarding public deficit, the prospects differ by case, mainly from the timing of return to primary balance stabilizing the public debt level in GDP.

i. The Central Account

The central account draws a gradual normalization of public finances' situation. The structural adjustment policy of the early period is relayed by the gradual output gap closure, which can eliminate public deficit's cyclical component. In total, the return to normal depends on the higher tax rate and a lot on the decline of the public expenditure's role in GDP.

Strong assumption, the early period restructuring policy does not affect economic growth to such an extent that additional fiscal effort is needed to position the deficit on the path that allows it to reach the public debt stabilizing level in GDP.

In the central account, the deficit decreases gradually. Compared to 2010, the decline is significant, due to a decline in public expenditure - public expenditure excluding interest expense drops a little more and tax revenue losses due to the crisis are erased. In the short term, the deficit decreases less. Essentially, this decline is accepted in the long term and in 6 years that the government balance stabilizing public debt influence in GDP will be achieved.

Reducing public deficit comes first from a structural adjustment policy. The structural deficit is declining. Moreover, the growth gap's gradual closing leads to the disappearance of the deficit's cyclical component, which will be reduced in the short term. Overall, the reduction of the different public deficits mainly through a decline in public expenditure, whose level relative to GDP would decline. The decline in public expenditure excluding debt interest would be somewhat higher; debt interest costs of would rise slightly while lowering from their peak.

iii. The other scenarios

In other scenarios, where revenue increased, in all cases like in the baseline scenario, changes in public finance will depend on the macroeconomic context drawn by both the potential growth perspectives, which serve as standard to primary and effective public expenditure's growth. The second scenario differs from the first by the early strong cyclical recovery in the context of assuming potential growth identical to the baseline scenario and the same fiscal policy. The growth deficit is filled sooner so that the cyclical deficit disappears faster.

This achievement reflects global public debt whose decline allows a greater public deficit reduction attributed to changes in the structural balance in accordance with normal accounting treatment of interest charges. The decline in public expenditure drawn in the baseline scenario is amplified in this second scenario by the savings on public debt interest costs permitted by reducing public debt level relative to what it is in the baseline scenario. The tax burden is constant, which is a quite conventional hypothesis: given the strong power of early cyclical recovery period, one could indeed expect a jump in revenue stronger than in the baseline scenario.

Of all scenarios, the third is the least favorable, both economically, since accumulated global growth losses are not recovered, and in terms of public finances. Indeed, the public deficit cyclical component is never filled. In addition, while the fiscal impulse is the same as in other cases - the primary public expenditure growing at the same rate, the tax burden is the same - the government balance does not stabilize public debt's weight in countries' GDP that increase with interest charges inflation effects.

As for the cyclical balance, what must be remembered is that it remains unchanged since the initial growth deficit is never reached. Moreover, the "cyclical" qualification of part of the public deficit is debatable since a prolonged initial growth gap led to this public deficit component, which effectively ceases to be cyclical and becomes structural.

Everything that happens in this scenario is as if the crisis had effectively reduced the growth potential. As for the structural balance, if the fiscal impulse in the early period causes a reduction in conditions close to the first two scenarios, it operates very differently beyond. The tax burden is the same as in the first two scenarios but, as regards public expenditure, its evolution is quite different. Public expenditure excluding interest expense grow at the same rate, but as economic growth is less favorable in the early period - it does not reach the level of potential output even though the growth rate is at the potential growth rate level - the weight of public expenditure, which only declined transiently, is still higher than in other scenarios. Besides the growth gap effects, there is the high incidence of interest charges inflation in a context of rising public debt in GDP ratio. At end of period, interests reach a GDP sensitive point, an increase which does more than offsetting the primary expenditure level decline.

The last two scenarios are built on the assumption of global potential growth slowdown, stronger in scenario 5 than scenario 4. Because of the sharp growth slowdown in Scenario 5, fiscal policy appears to be less "restrictive" structural adjustment is less important - than in scenario 4, the latter itself being less strong than in the baseline scenario. This result reflects the fact that early period structural adjustment "burden" is much lighter, in terms of structural deficit reduction, since potential growth is lower. However, in these two scenarios, the cyclical balance is balanced, what's the more quickly since potential growth is low.

Ultimately, maintaining a higher structural deficit in scenario 5 of slower growth is accompanied by a stronger public deficit, the scenario 5's structural effort deficit outweighing the loss, faster in this scenario, of the cyclical deficit.

This illustrates the idea that for the same public expenditure growth rate there is a correspondingly different structural fiscal adjustment depending on the potential growth rate. The higher it is, the more the effort stands out as such and vice versa. The future potential growth level issue being particularly debated today, Scenarios 4 and 5's comparative results combined with those of the baseline scenario have the advantage of measuring the impact of a possible potential growth slowdown and its effect on public accounts in the context of a given fiscal policy.

In this case, public expenditure growth relates to potential growth respective levels except at the early period, when the fiscal impulse in public finances' medium term programming is assumed. Despite an identical effort to control public expenditure, that structural effort emerges as less effective in the more sharply slowed potential growth scenario than in the scenario where the slowdown is less marked. Is also raised the question of the appropriateness of a given fiscal policy configuration to different growth contexts of marked by more or less strong potential growth momentum to come.

2. *The public debt trajectories*

Public debt trajectories associated with the different scenarios are also strongly contrasting but only the scenario 3 (which is the worst case scenario) has uncontrolled changes in the level of non-public debt. The long term fiscal policy is the same in all scenarios but public expenditures increase even less since the potential growth hypothesis is weak.

In scenario 3, the public balance does not reach the level that would stabilize public debt's weight in GDP despite the early period structural adjustment. The public debt dynamics is exacerbated by the gap between the economic growth rate and the cost of public debt.

In contrast with this scenario, the others show that public debt, despite its sharp increase in the crisis, is not installed on an explosive path so that, under certain economic conditions, fiscal policy, even neutral, may be accompanied by stabilization, or even a fairly sharp decline, of public debt's burden in GDP.

In the baseline scenario, public deficit's evolution implies an increase in public debt down to 6 years. Despite fairly strong growth, up to that date, public deficit does not reach the level required to stabilize the public debt / GDP ratio. However, beyond that date, public debt is reduced and this leads to lower GDP, interest charges causing a reduction of total public expenditure larger than for primary spending.

This is the scenario of strong cyclical recovery that allows the reflux of the largest public debt. But most scenarios, which differ by the long term growth rate level but are similar in terms of short-term recovery, setting public debt in the range of 80 GDP percentage points.

C. Arbitration between growth and fiscal adjustment

The current global situation is characterized by a dilemma: how to arbitrate between growth and fiscal adjustment? The conditions of this arbitration - the multiplicity of actors involved - increasing the difficulties encountered. In addition, long-term considerations related to aging are interfering with the "end of crisis" agenda.

I. Public debt's mechanics

The different public finances scenarios, of which we just presented the results, illustrate the lessons of a relatively simple theoretical analysis framework that identifies the determinants of public debt dynamics.

Under initial debt conditions and fixed economic growth, it is possible to stabilize the public debt level in GDP. This balance is such that it equalizes public debt increase and GDP growth. It is therefore equal to the difference between the product of the initial debt by the economic growth rate and the initial debt.

One can deduce from this equation some arithmetic observations, some of which are reassuring but should be supplemented by more economic data and both more relevant and more worrying for countries where the public debt level reaches an unsustainable level.

1. *Two arithmetic observations*

i. *The public debt paradox*

Arithmetically, the higher the initial public debt level, the higher, with a given growth rate, the public balance stabilizing public debt may be. Consider two cases with a public debt of 25% of GDP in the first and 50% of GDP in the second and a GDP growth of 5% in value in both cases, the balance stabilizing public debt corresponds to a deficit of 1.25 GDP percentage point in the first case, and in the second, 2.5 GDP percentage points.

This arithmetic sequence, which represents a kind of "debt paradox", invites us to observe that two countries with identical deficit goals in the same growth context will experience different public debts trajectories, according to its initial level, if they have contrasting debt situations.

In such a case, it is the most indebted country that relieves the most debt. Thus, institutional agreements, implement, *a fortiori*, asymmetric financial discipline whose logic can be variously assessed, in terms of both public debt reduction programs efficiency and equity.

ii. *Debt derivative, GDP derivative*

Still arithmetically, stronger economic growth implies a higher balance to stabilize public debt. Assuming an initial public debt of 50% of GDP, if the public deficit must not exceed 2.5 percentage points of GDP when growth reached 5%, it can reach 5 GDP percentage points if it is 10%.

2. *Some considerations on the economic and financial assessment of high public debt circumstances*

These arithmetic observations must be supplemented by more economical considerations. While it is true that a country, where the public debt burden is relatively high, can stabilize it with a public deficit itself comparatively high, this arithmetic finding does not mean that it is easier to achieve this stabilizing balance.

We may first observe that the public debt level depends on a given accumulation of deficits after which the debt has grown more than the gross domestic product. In other words, between two countries with different public debt levels, the one where it is the highest is the one having the strongest gap between public debt growth and economic growth. It is possible that, for such countries, the effort needed to return to a debt trajectory parallel to GDP's is also the most demanding. However, this is not a certainty for at least two reasons.

First, the debt increase can be used to acquire transferable assets. Monitoring gross debt alone proved insufficient to assess States' financial situation. The ongoing crisis that has resulted in equity investments - in various forms - in businesses by Governments shows that there may be various configurations of assets net debt variations for a given gross debt variation.

Secondly, even if there is no direct counterpart in public debt in terms of assets, public debt finances public expenditures, or results in tax cuts, whose effect on economic growth must be taken into account. This obviously is crucial. In theory, a public debt increase shows that public deficits accumulate more than GDP; in other words, this means that public deficit's multiplier effect is, in the long term, lower at unit (the additional product is lower than the deficit).

However, two situations which might challenge this conclusion should, strictly speaking, be considered:

- Assuming that the growth deficit comes from other mechanisms whose correction would restore fiscal policy's economic efficiency;
- Assuming that the immediate economic return from a deficit would be lower at unit, but where it is cumulative, or delayed, yield would be equal or greater.

To illustrate these two scenarios, one may consider, in the first case, for example, possibly upsetting monetary policy effects (though many other variables can be considered) and in the second case, education expenses whose performance may be delayed (but many other public interventions can be involved) or tax deductions that could raise the private investment level.

Anyway, what is at stake is the economic viability of public interventions financed by loans. Given public interventions' potential importance in the future, it seems a high priority to progress in knowledge of its interventions' induced effects. In this connection, attaching to the budgetary surveillance more considerations for "public finances' quality" should be encouraged.

In addition, the higher is initial debt, the higher the risk of incurring the "snowball effect" of debt is important and the more it has serious consequences. Debt's snowball effect is the autonomous public deficit worsening process resulting from a discrepancy between the economic growth rate and the cost of debt associated with a given interest rates level.

When GDP's nominal growth rate is lower than debt's apparent interest rate, government debt tends to increase as a result of a self-sustaining process, interest expenses in turn lead to increases in the deficit which increases again the debt burden.

In other words, beyond the apparent facilities offered by a relatively high public debt level to a State starting to stabilize, the real degree of effort to undertake, in terms of primary balance, should consider budgetary discipline tightening involved, in that event, by initiation of a "snowball effect".

The danger is that relatively high public debt levels expose a configuration where this effect can be triggered. From this point of view, if we cannot say that as debt increases interest rates must rise, then it must be emphasized that the risk of tension on the interest rate itself increases in this case and that the destabilizing effects of such tension also worsen. There is obviously no automatic link between the public debt level and the interest rates level charged on public loans. The crisis has caused a considerable public debt increase.

Meanwhile, interest rates attached to new loans are historically low. These phenomena are suspected to be due to a "flight to quality", which allows funding public debt cheaply. But even without such a process, the correlation between public debt's derivative and sovereign bond market rate is no more than very loose. Moreover, it is often true that, at equal debt levels, an economy where public debt's share is relatively higher experiences more favorable monetary conditions. Under normal circumstances, sovereign risk is less "expensive" than private agents' risks.

The fact remains that it is imperative to consider the financial risk incurred by a government whose public finances' configuration leads to a continuous rise in public debt. The danger is obviously that this government encounters financial difficulties, either loaners turn away from the shares it issues, or they impose higher interest rates. In the latter case, different from a solvency crisis, which is the summary of the first, the gap between the cost of debt and growth exacerbates debt's snowball effect and raises the fiscal consolidation constraint. There should be a primary balance still higher than necessary to stabilize debt before the tension on the loan conditions. Current events show that markets can impose increasingly strained monetary conditions on some states. Similarly, history does not exclude solvency crises.

II. A tradeoff between fiscal adjustment and economic growth

The deficit level now seems inconsistent with public debt stabilization and even more with its return to the Stability and Growth Pact target level. However, the possibility of a non-controlled evolution of global public debt seems to have to be regarded as a hypothesis: that the initial growth deficit would never be filled, this even if fiscal policy simulated for the long term should be neutral.

In other words, even without applying tight fiscal discipline in the future, countries' public debt shifted more or less rapidly. These perspectives regrettably do not inform on the degree of public debt escalation risk. The worst case scenario, no more than the other, is not strictly probable. In particular, the question arises whether the medium term planned fiscal stance, which is a condition of consistency of the longer term scenarios, will not have an adverse effect on growth, because of its restrictive stance.

The latter question reflects the arbitration terms forced by the current economic and financial situation:

- Implementing a public deficit reduction policy could weigh on growth;
- Eliminating this risk by adopting a neutral or expansionary fiscal policy puts them at risk of a public debt structural increase that ultimately strengthen the financial recovery requirements.

Method warning

A prior method warning is needed here. Some economists argue that, far from weighing on growth prospects, fiscal policies to reduce public deficits exert a favorable effect on economic growth even in the short term. Before the crisis, quite a number of studies in this direction have been published. One can even say that these studies were the substrata influencing the majority doctrine. It is now possible to consider that this view is a little backward. We hardly find evidence of this kind in the literature since the global crisis erupted. No doubt however that, rightly or wrongly, the time will come when this view, once dominant, will reappear. However, we must face the facts: the idea that fiscal policies for large and rapid public deficits reduction could be conducted without risk to growth in the short term is no longer present in the public decision landscape.

Economic policy implementation is necessary: it must be a policy resolutely towards reducing public deficits, since this policy is not only prudent but also carries benefits for growth. In short, under this view, the trade-off between growth and public deficits reduction evoked here is a red herring.

Scenario 3 illustrates the risks to public finances in the imagined fiscal policy pattern. In this scenario where, after the early period structural adjustment, a neutral fiscal policy would be carried out, economic growth is insufficient to ensure that, at the public balance level reached, the debt is under control.

This risk can be averted at the cost of a more restrictive fiscal policy. But the gap between effective balance and the balance stabilizing debt in this scenario, a gap that is growing because of interest expenses dynamic increase is high and is a measure of fiscal adjustment that should be undertaken in this case.

It should set a tight budget for a lower long term public deficit so that global public debt stabilizes. Such a fiscal result implies twice the effort ex ante given the budgetary constraints short term effects.

In a variant of the baseline scenario described above, fiscal policy is tightened. Public debt by country would be alleviated in view of the central account by a high amputation of the short term growth. The end of crisis could be delayed, which, in turn, could affect the long term growth prospects - potential growth – of global economy. This variant emphasizes fiscal prudence at the expense of growth.

The various scenarios explored lead to question the necessity of this choice. Their first lesson is, indeed, rather comforting: except in the case where the potential output gap widened during the crisis is never made up, the fiscal policy, even if neutral at the end - that is to say it would not seek any structural adjustment - does confine countries' debt into "reasonable" limits.

Thus, the crisis fiscal legacy would be very worrying only if its economic legacy - the output gap – was to continue. This first lesson implies a second: short-term economic trends are likely to influence countries' fiscal position into the future, i.e., the recovery pattern is important.

In the worst case scenario, economic growth is on average, over the long term, greater than it is in one of the other scenarios. Yet, with identical fiscal policy, public debt escalation is high in scenario 3 and absent in scenario 5. The difference between the two situations is the growth rate during the initial period: it is higher in scenario 5 and this helps containing the early period public debt growth.

This difference implies higher interest rates in Scenario 3 and, consequently, an increased level of the critical gap between public balance and the one stabilizing public debt in GDP. In scenario 3, debt emerges and steadily increases. The initial impact on economic growth is also illustrated by the comparison between the first two scenarios. In the long term, growth is the same but it is stronger in scenario 2 where the output gap is filled faster than the baseline scenario.

It is therefore essential to foster economic recovery as fast and as strong as possible if the desire is to prevent public debt's increase that would complicate long-term control. A third lesson follows. Assuming that the risk of stifling economic recovery increases with the intensity of fiscal consolidation, avoid excesses in this area. Fiscal adjustment in the medium term, contributes positively to the long term global debt trajectory. It draws a policy with acceptable realism giving prospect of an international public debt. Scenario 2 shows that if the recovery would be stronger, that policy would result in a faster return to levels of debt lower. Only in scenario 3 is this policy insufficient.

To control public debt in the world, fiscal policy tightening is necessary if one takes as a basis that it is the most likely economic scenario. Is it advisable to make that choice? It seems that the precautionary principle applied to economic policies lead to answer this question in the negative. And a similar answer is appropriate in terms of fiscal policy.

First, assuming that the production potential will not be reached in the short term and therefore that it must tighten fiscal policy would have two major drawbacks:

- The first, known as self-fulfilling expectations, is to adopt a fiscal policy that weighs on the recovery leading subsequently to the situation feared ex ante;

- The second is to reduce economies' potential growth rate in which it would probably depend on the timing of economic recovery. Scenarios 4 and 5 show that, in this case, debt would flow back less than if the growth potential was preserved.

On the other hand, the fiscal policy tightening variant shows that this option could be at any time, effectively mobilized to control public debt if the economic recovery would remain sluggish. There is thus an asymmetry in the two fiscal policies considered: excessive fiscal policy tightening may have irreversible effects that a more pragmatic approach avoids.

CHAPTER 10

Necessary Economic Policies Cooperation

This period's difficulties are compounded by the need for coordination across a multiplicity of actors. Besides the challenge of monitoring economic growth patterns' sustainability to preserve public finances from future shocks as great as what they face in the current global crisis, two forms of coordination should be considered for end of crisis period.

A. Economic policies coordination

The fiscal and monetary policies combination is a first challenge. In the scenarios, interest rates are conventionally fixed at their current level corresponding to a monetary policy and accommodative financial conditions. As an alternative to the baseline scenario, we measure the effects of a rise above public debt apparent rates.

The cost of debt carries a risk premium which causes public loans increase by 1 point. It follows a sharp interest expense increase and a lesser improvement in public deficit (4% of GDP in 2030). Public debt increases by 21 GDP percentage points in 2030 and settles at 103 GDP percentage points. Public debt increase would be larger if these models also simulated interest rates tension's restrictive effect on economic growth.

This variant appears to teach two lessons:

- First, it is desirable that monetary policy is grounded by looking for a strong and rapid economic recovery and a in cooperation with the fiscal authorities;
- They should strengthen the monetary authorities by implementing credible fiscal policy for return to financial positions compatible with public debt markets equilibrium without pressure on interest rates.

B. Fiscal policies coordination

Most countries are facing deteriorating fiscal situations likely to lead to non-controllable public debt changes. At the same time, general budgetary positions analysis framework applied here to France also applies to them. Only in the event of a too slow and too weak economic recovery would budgetary guidelines implying a gradual and measured public finances recovery prove to be inadequate for handling public debt.

In this configuration, there is a risk: that each country adopts a heavily restrictive fiscal policy relying on the fact that the neighbors will favor, for their part, the rapid return to strong growth likely to offset the effects of its domestic fiscal contraction.

In this configuration all countries would in fact adopt the same overly restrictive policy with adverse consequences for economic growth.

The other risk, conversely, is that everyone imagines that other states will make efforts that exempt it from implementing the guidelines necessary for its finances' control. This risk, the stowaway behavior, seems quite unlikely given the new financial deal. The latter differs from the previous one by a reassessment of financial risks and the likelihood of a now strong enough international financial markets reshaping becoming less conducive to financial "recycling" of current imbalances in the world.

The first risk is higher. To avert its occurrence, it is desirable that fiscal policy coordination is institutionalized and inspired by the desire to implement more cooperative policies. This would establish orderly standardization programs for global public finances taking into account national circumstances and greater or lesser distance from sustainable financial positions. This would require considerable progress in macroeconomic and macro-financial regulation.

C. The issue of "aging" population effects on Western public finances

Ageing should result in public expenditure increases but in very different proportions in different countries.

Several countries will experience a greater public expenditure increase. These projections depend on general growth scenarios and the action of assumptions necessary to project the different categories of expenditure sensitive to ageing, given that these projections are made with the current rules in place. It is estimated, in general, the higher growth will be, the less public expenditure increase related to ageing will be strong.

We must not however lean overbroad in that observation. A large number of expenses related to age relate to the economic growth rate. This is moreover a direction, discussed as such, of social protection policies, to loosen the link between social spending and growth, which as it is, remains fairly tight.

The fact remains that the financing costs needed to cover additional expenses due to aging will not be as acute, whether that growth will allow or not gaining purchasing power to assets and capital owners.

In the general context drawn by the demographic projections of a working age population decline is offset by higher employment rate (a higher percentage of the workforce would be employed) and neutralizing the adverse demographic trends in the number of hours worked, potential economic growth would slow in most countries.

Gains in productivity per hour, slowing compared to long-term trends, would provide in the future, the greatest growth potential. In most countries, employment is still rising, weakly contributing to growth potential. However, in few countries, the outlook would reduce the unfavorable demographic growth potential compared to the expectations related to gains in labor productivity. In yet others, potential growth will be achieved through productivity gains and increased time remaining in employment. Growth will, in the future, dependent on productivity gains.

On this point, we must first recall that the long term prospects are subject to considerable uncertainty. In addition, it may be noted that productivity projections on the whole expect similar gains for most developed countries. If differences, still possible - given the maintenance, or even widening, of strong enough national specificities in the productive capacity composition and investment dynamics in particular -, were involved, countries will probably experience more contrasting changes in age-related expenditures dynamics.

Ageing exerts its effects mainly through increasing the pensioners' share in the population. This "demographic ratio" is expected to deteriorate, the dependency ratio relating the population aged over 65 years to 15-64 years-old people will substantially grow in the next decade. A study has been conducted to measure the long-term impact of additional public expenditure arising from aging population.

Under the condition that additional annual public expenditure over the period averaging 0.3 points of GDP is not funded, this variant causes a higher growth but increased structural deficit and public debt. It reaches at least a level greater by 19.4 GDP percentage points than in the baseline scenario, around 100 points of GDP over the long term. At a longer horizon, the adjustment need for the structural balance due to aging population is stronger. For some countries, the aging population burden has even more requirements.

PART FOUR

Global Authorities Residency

CHAPTER 11

A Relatively Intact Global Economy Despite Countries' Deteriorating Public Accounts

The crisis has an ambivalent impact on the global economic outlook. On the one hand, it further weakens public accounts already undermined by years of deficits; on the other, it tends to undermine a number of situations apparently gained from globalization: the rebirth of some countries as economic superpowers, even the emergence of new "dragon", now seems in doubt. Should it, for all that, consider that countries, whose state economic model has emerged stronger in many respects, will emerge relatively stronger from the crisis? This is doubtful. For the same reasons that led these states to be less affected than others by the crisis are also likely to result in a sustained decrease both of the potential growth level and the rate of expansion of their economies, when they will have to provide resources to handle an increasingly burdensome debt.

A. Should the recovery plan be revived?

I. Update on the recovery plan in the world

The global public finance direction should be an opportunity to review the concrete implementation of the recovery plan measures, both in terms of "engineering" used in the world to ensure their implementation, and effective injection of funds into the economy.

The main recovery plan measures

The revenue constituent: $ 17 billion is spent on average by countries in corporate treasury support, through the monthly consumer loans repayments, accelerated research tax credit debts repayment, corporate tax losses carryback repayment and corporation tax excess payments' refund. Moreover, 3 billion on average in G7 countries are dedicated to exceptional reduction of income taxes paid worldwide to support low incomes tax households' purchasing power and consumption. Public investment programs across the world include credit for countries' investment and equipment expenditures: this is usually the acceleration of projects already identified in civilian infrastructures and facilities, higher education and research, defense and security equipment and heritage. The support program for economic activity and employment is destined to finance all corporate investment and employment measures, as well as the endowment for the strategic investment fund. The effort for housing and global solidarity is devoted to measures for housing and urban renewal and for financing the active solidarity premium.

In some countries, local governments have pledged to maintain their investment level despite the crisis, thus benefiting from early repayment of several compensation funds. These measures will enhance their investment section's revenue. Measures' implementation resulted in signing agreements with operators, enterprises and local governments involved in these countries. With regard to budgetary allocations, and according to the expenses' nature, the implementation in other countries takes place either by transfer to existing programs of the general budget, or through mission programs' direct management. In case of transfer, credits traceability is ensured through an appropriate implementation nomenclature, each transfers recipient program being provided with sub-actions dedicated to the recovery plan.

These elements call for two remarks:

1. With respect to budget appropriations, i.e. on average only one-fifth of total payment credits for the mission in the world. The recovery plan consumption rate will increase in most of the world, especially by starting a hundred yards of new transport and security setting infrastructure at the universities.
2. The amount of investment expected from local authorities is considerable, given the average investment observed in previous years.

B. Are additional measures needed?

The deficit in the short and medium term could be even higher if countries were to decide on additional stimulus measures, so as not to break recovery by a negative fiscal impulse. Indeed, it is not the deficit in itself which may circumstantially support growth, but the fiscal impulse, i.e. its increase. The fact that countries' public deficit was positive offered, as such, no support to growth. If in a given year, actually applied stimulus amounting to one percent of GDP, and if almost all these measures' effects are felt upon the year in question, then the failure to extend these measures the following year cuts growth from an amount equivalent to the first year's increase.

However, the global stimulus could take its toll more slowly because of the time required for the expenditure and distribution of their impact in the economy. Moreover, some countries reforms could significantly increase local authorities' investment in the coming years. This increase was not reflected in global stimulus plans funds as originally assessed. These measures are indeed valued in proportion to their cost to the government.

C. Long-term scenarios

I. Probably definitely reduced GDP

1. In the short term, a probably permanent potential GDP reduction

The current crisis is not an ordinary economic crisis but a banking crisis which, like other serious banking crises, will have a permanent impact on GDP. As only a portion, probably limited, of the debts will be paid and as part of countries' communities has not signed the convention, it is unclear whether all communities' expenditures are very different, despite the importance of investment forecasts.

Usually, GDP growth in the world fluctuates around a long-term trend. This trend is structural because it depends on demographics and labor productivity growth, which is itself the result of investment and of total factor productivity growth. Growth below potential in a given year is thus normally offset by growth higher than potential in subsequent years.

Serious banking crises prevent this mechanism from working, creating an investment backlog that is not subsequently caught up: a permanent reduction of several points. The fact that catching up will not begin until later probably comes from banking crisis core feature, which prevents growth from being above potential, then the agents cannot spend more than they earn. Although a permanent reduction in potential GDP may seem high, it is not likely.

A key challenge for public finances

If one considers that global GDP may be structurally reduced, this means that the cyclical part of the deficit also lowers, while its structural part increases: three attitudes are possible:

- Either we accept a sudden loss of potential GDP;
- Or we refuse to accept any loss of potential GDP;

- Or we adopt an intermediate position of considering the potential GDP in the world is indeed reduced, but this reduction is "smoothed" over time.

There is growth potential for the global economy in the short term so the contraction would result in a widening output gap, which is based on a cautious assumption of a recovery in GDP growth at a rate higher than global economy's growth potential. Under these cautious assumptions, the output gap would still grow in the short term. If one accepts that the current low or negative growth corresponds in part to a sudden and final loss of GDP, output gap will be eliminated over time. The government structural balance will be equal to the effective balance. Reducing the structural deficit would then still be below the target set by States in excessive deficit.

If however we refuse to admit the finality of the loss of GDP, the implications in terms of structural balance results become so disconnected from the effective balance that they become absurd.

For an effective balance, which would of course be the same, it would result in a long-term structural balance. The apparent structural deficit reduction would be, for its part, significant in the short term, whereas, in fact, GDP would move away from its potential displayed in the world.

2. *A sustainable risk reduction in potential growth rate*

Some consider that this might be the case, due to a reduction in total factor productivity growth, resulting for example from a greater risk aversion to provoke a small investment, or loss of sustainable human capital. In practice, however, historically major banking crises were not followed by a potential growth reduction, but on the contrary, and paradoxically, by its acceleration: this risk forbids reducing the deficit by increasing tax burden.

II. *Global public debt likely to stabilize at around 100 points of GDP*

Regardless of the possible crisis consequences, global economic potential growth should be slightly reduced in the next few years: the impact on the global debt burden of a possible rise in interest rates would be offset by a corresponding reduction of other expenditures. If, in the world, governments were complying only with a target primary balance, a higher interest rate could increase public debt to nearly 200 points of GDP. The global debt snowball effect scenario implies a higher public debt apparent interest rate.

Scenarios with snowball effect are often presented in a didactic purpose, to warn against a policy that would leave the debt burden drift to fuel itself. They, however, have the drawback of assuming that governments will allow their total deficits to achieve a sustainably very high level, which hardly seems realistic. The scenario without the snowball effect, however, shows that the risk of a global public debt remaining at a level close to 100 points of GDP beyond the short term is credible. The current crisis would, thus, have a lasting impact on public finances in most countries.

Overall, global interest rates cannot sustainably stay above the long term growth rate. Sooner or later re-balancing mechanisms will be implemented. But they are not effective in some countries' case, which may be faced with interest rates levels calibrated for economies growing faster. These countries' economy risks being dragged into a low growth vicious circle insofar as to cope with relatively high interest rates laid by their markets, they should increase their taxes on long-term investments necessary for their growth, competitiveness and thus to maintain their standard of living.

III. Ensuring economic and social sustainability

The current crisis by its violence is a litmus test for global economies. Some of them are already known or will be too fragile to weather the storm without lasting harm; others may even sink, and in consequence, risk destabilizing other economies associated with them. When one sees accumulating both acute risks relating to the financial situation of any country and the overall uncertainties regarding large countries' ability to control their money's long-term growth without affecting the recovery chances, it is important to define a rigorous and courageous strategy, if we do not want the overall confidence to wilt.

Controlling expenditure through saving revenue, preparing to take decisions as tough as inevitable, socially speaking, are the pillars of the strategy, which requires special attention to the countries' access conditions to financial markets. Yesterday, it was the currency exchange rate which was an indicator of market sentiment on the global economy health; today, interest rate spreads between countries have this function and must be monitored. But unlike previous years, the market pressure on government bond rates alone no longer, necessarily, has the result of exchange rate changes that will expedite the resolution of imbalances, but a higher cost of debt.

D. Controlling expenditure and saving the revenue even in crisis

I. Continued structural reforms, a new form of ardent obligation during the crisis

1. An underutilized savings potential

In a difficult economic context, countries should take note of falling revenue, and make, about expenditures, a courageous strategic choice: not to use the crisis as a pretext to abandon, in the name of the recovery, any budgetary discipline, and to continue efforts to control state spending. In fact, the extremely erratic inflation changes will, in the short term, greatly complicate expenditure control in most countries. Expected to decline, inflation, on annual average, causes a sudden increase in the indexed debt burden and maybe responsible for the expenditure escalation during that year in the world.

The crisis is causing a significant increase of some expenditure items, particularly in the area of employment and means-tested benefits. For some missions, the increased expenditure is of such magnitude in view of the mission ceiling that excess envelope funding was unthinkable. However, other missions have their ceiling often raised as a result of new directions in government policy. These revaluations are partially absorbed by the mobilization of the budgeting reserve, as evidenced by missions' ceilings decrease in the majority of countries.

The detailed purpose for these overruns concern the increased aid to disabled adults, single parents, housing allowances, loans for emergency housing, asylum in most countries. In total, and given all these revaluations, one can do nothing but regret that the maximum benefit was not gained from the potential savings generated by low inflation. The remark is also in the medium term: when prices increase will find a higher level, the opposite effect will occur and will impose rising pressure on expenditure.

2. A significant downsizing effort

In terms of public expenditure in general and staff costs in particular, the multiplication of governments' operators is nevertheless a vantage point to watch. Declining enrollment paid directly by the states must be assessed taking also into account the fact that the major governments' operators, which contribute to public policies' implementation and, for many, who enjoy state subsidies, saw their number grow very rapidly in recent years. Operators across the country are also involved in this effort (downsizing). This orientation is commendable but its implementation details should be clarified during the discussions.

II. The need to expand expenditure control efforts after the crisis

3. Sill high upward pressure on Government expenditure around the world

Lower inflation expectations should allow the Government to make significant savings. Conversely, the economic recovery, in all likelihood, will be accompanied by an inflation resurgence.

Government expenditure will first undergo a strong upward pressure due to increased debt burden. Starting this year, the debt burden is indeed likely to increase sharply due to their current stock increase (volume effect), but also the interest rates and inflation increase that are sure to follow from the economic recovery.

Other major increase factors remain:

1. In pensions expenditure, whose average annual growth expected over the short term establishes in billions of dollars, reflecting the large number of civil servants retirement and pensions revaluations that will result from inflation;
2. In the evolution of levies on earnings, levy revenue growth for countries' local authorities follows the inflation pace. The levy on revenue to the global benefit could experience an even more dynamic increase, especially due to the significant budget expenditure increase by country.

Based on the assumptions, let us develop two extreme public expenditure evolution scenarios:

1. In the optimistic scenario, debt burden, pensions, and levies on revenue expenditures increase each year in volume at

minimum. Other expenses decrease to the maximum and staff costs are stable;

2. In the pessimistic scenario, the rate of volume increase of debt burden, pensions, personnel and levies on revenue expenditures is set at the maximum level provided by countries. Other expenditures know a volume decline rate lower than expected.

2. *Towards widespread intervention adjustments on policy*

All of the above makes it even more crucial to restrain expenditure, which should involve substantial adjustments. One of the main challenges of these reforms' second phase per country will be to define the reforms that will generate the savings needed to control current expenditure.

On this point, expenditure trends analysis offers an interesting lesson. Indeed, the main variable of downward Government expenditure adjustment in the short term lies in the category: other expenses, including annual average growth should be negative in billions of dollars per country. This category includes State investment, its operating costs, subsidies to operators, the benefits on the counter provided by states, endowments governed by legislation and other interventions in each country. This pool of savings amounted in total to billions of dollars or one third of global average budget.

Other expenses: only source of savings.

This category includes expenditure of very diverse nature with varying degrees of rigidity. Regarding annual expenditure control, the room for maneuver is, in particular, greatly limited for expenditures covered by laws or indexed, such as endowment to government, loans to out of revenue local authorities or balancing subsidies paid by some states to special pension regimes. To the current law, the savings potential is also low on wicket interventions, which meet social rights held by households and are most often indexed, as well as subsidies for public service expenses of operators, which fund mainly staff costs and operating numerous satellite states.

These elements therefore demonstrate that the savings pool glimpsed in the other expenses category cannot be mobilized at the cost of ambitious structural reforms and policies for intervention.

CHAPTER 12

Saving Revenue: an Uncompromising Imperative, Given the Likely Low GDP Elasticity of Government Revenue

A. The slowdown in the buoyant revenue relative to GDP

We need to emphasize that the important parameter of revenue elasticity relative to GDP. In particular, insist that this elasticity in the long term should be - on current law - close to unit. It follows that the high rates recorded in recent years, should be matched, in a low cycle phase, with a revenue growth rate below that of the economy and that this will affect both government revenue and the various countries' Social Security.

Social contributions in most countries rely on earned income which not only shrink in recession but usually grows more slowly than GDP in recovery. As for tax revenue elasticity, which was particularly high in recent years in some countries, it could now be substantially less than unit. Furthermore, it should take into account discretionary measures' impact as an opportunity for companies to carry forward their tax losses, which represents, over the long term, potential corporate taxes loss of several dozen billion.

B. Being vigilant at all times in public debt

If crisis and global stimulus measures will, on first analysis, have no more than a temporary impact on sales, it will not be the same on debt, whose massive increase will require a long and sustained reduction effort. Under these conditions, increased vigilance on the debt goes today through a correct anticipation of the effects of its increase on future balances as well as improved information about the conditions of its funding.

I. The issues of government securities proliferation

1. Interest rates: States in the "eye of the storm"

Through central banks' intervention, rates at short and medium term declined *a priori* without precedent in the recent monetary history. Interest rates at 1 year decreased significantly. Even if one finds, for maturities greater than or equal to three years, a tendency to catch up, this is expected, given central banks' attitude. The whole question is how long can this be sustained?

For now, banks tend, given enterprises' weak credit demand, to invest plenty of cash they hold in government bonds, because they desire to avoid using extra capital. This propensity would prevent long rates' increase despite public deficits. Moreover, companies are showing such a preference for liquidity that they are willing to settle for extremely low pay, even symbolic, to maintain full availability of their assets. But sooner or later this exceptional situation should end.

2. *Global debt sustainability*

The risks associated with excessive public debt are well known. The increase in debt comes first with a rise in its burden, which reduces future fiscal policy's leeway and its ability for a countercyclical influence in the short term.

Secondly, the abundance of sovereign debt may lead to crowding out private investment, since public and private borrowers are in competition in the loanable funds market. This leads to higher interest rates, when the increased supply of government securities results in lower prices and obliges States to pay higher rates to attract new lenders. This rise may, moreover increase if borrowers come to doubt the Government's ability to pay its due in the future, leading to a risk premium increase.

In a context where States' public debt could reach 79.7% of GDP on average, in turn, interest charges could reach 3.7% in the short term if the debt was 90% of national wealth. Debt levels, reflecting stimulus financing in the world, today clearly pose the question of a possible debt runaway and medium-term public finances' sustainability. Note that sustainability is the situation of a Government whose solvency is assured without having a particular need to adjust its fiscal policy in the future. The lack of public finances' sustainability is diagnosed when compliance with the intertemporal budget constraint is no longer possible without significant adjustments to revenues or expenditures. Such a scenario is not a figment of the imagination, and public debt rapid rise should be considered as an option in some countries. Thus, on the basis of a debt equal to 80% of GDP and a 1.5 point difference between interest rate and growth rate, a widening of the primary deficit by 0.1 percentage points per year would lead to a debt level of 100% of GDP over the medium term. Global public debt: is the trend of the last twenty years sustainable?

In these circumstances it is reasonable to ask at what debt level countries' credibility would be undermined, resulting in an increase in the risk premium to serve investors and consequently the interest burden to supporting taxpayers.

At this stage, the three rating agencies (Fitch Ratings, Moody's and Standard & Poor's) assign an AAA grade, the highest level, to public debt in most G7 countries. The rating outlook is stable among the three agencies, despite the rise in public debt comes from measures to support the economy and the financial sector. These measures are indeed perceived as necessary to cushion the crisis effects and preserve these countries' financial sector soundness, and not to let them be considered by agencies as a source of concern in the short term. Nevertheless, they pay close attention to the end of crisis conditions, for countries, as well as action to restore public finances' balance.

The crucial question will be how the much more proportionally indebted the States' ability to embark on the path of debt after the crisis. In this regard, developed countries reflect a tradition of increasing the public debt followed by stabilization, rather than recession. Finally, based on financial indicators and States' adjustment capacity, Moody's places among others Germany, Canada and Scandinavia in the stronger group. These countries have a very good capacity for economic adjustment, taking into account the diversification of their economies, the low volatility of these industrial and leadership measured by the cumulative size, relative to GDP among their enterprises the 500 largest. Some of these countries scores are, however, down the criteria for global competitiveness and innovation, which deserves consideration.

CONCLUSION

Following this overview of the global economy, it is useful to be a little less pessimistic. The Global economy is forecasted to experience a particularly dark and uncertain start point. If economic policies have limited the extent of the recession, it is not certain that recovery will be strong or sustained. Once this is finished, during the removal period, consumption may suffer internal stimulus loss of impetus, external demand weakening and rising unemployment.

Thus, a strong and rapid economic recovery which, however, limits the crisis' lasting effects is far from certain and the uncertainty is reinforced by structural imbalances thrown in broad daylight by the crisis. On this last point, the crisis first showed excess liquidity dangers, still relevant after several months of accommodative monetary policy, now looking for "exit strategies".

Moreover, the mismatch between supply and demand plans could persist if a reflection on the distribution of value added and the growing dispersion of wages was not engaged.

Finally, the main global imbalances remain. It appears that, particularly at the global level, the risk of a severe adjustment in exchange rates cannot be ruled out while at regional level, the coexistence of antagonistic national growth models creates fault lines whose consequences continue to be underestimated. Thus, the coexistence of growth based on household consumption and growth dependent on external competitiveness gains, boosted by a competitive disinflation wage policy, may seem winning in the short term to some countries, but in the long term it is a “lose-lose” strategy for global growth.

It is not clear if the crisis would have a lasting impact on the global economy growth rate, the potential growth concept is at the heart of this problem. However, the calculation of potential growth is particularly uncertain, especially in the context of a sharp slowdown in activity. On this point, the current crisis will have a lasting negative impact on potential growth in most major industrialized countries due to falling investment and rising structural unemployment mainly due to the loss of employability that caused by a prolonged vacancy. But it would be dangerous to adopt, on this basis alone, economic policies that could, by being too austere, precipitate the economic sequences and ultimately delay the end of crisis.

In contrast, potential growth is suitable for estimating long term global economy growth. Thus, in our five scenarios, the first three retain a potential growth hypothesis, and its stronger or lesser decrease.

Macroeconomic outcomes associated with these scenarios are clearly contrasted: they show that increasing the potential growth is a major issue. It is the only likely to allow gains in household purchasing power, living standards improvement and reducing tensions over income distribution in particular between workers and pensioners, which are expected to increase in future.

In these circumstances, there is no real alternative but to improve economic efficiency by seeking to productivity gains maximization, which goes through growth policies favoring training, research and innovation. The various scenarios enlighten the short-term choices testing the effects on public debt of five well-differentiated economic configurations. For this exercise to keep all its purpose, fiscal policy whose effects are estimated is, in all scenarios, the same. Thus, the set of scenarios allow measuring public finances' sensitivity to the short term conditions - what recovery? – and to differences between potential growth perspectives.

The first lesson of this exercise is that, except in the worst case scenario, fiscal policy results in a tight grip on public debt. In particular, in the baseline scenario, debt experiences a peak and then flows back in the long term. The results of the first two scenarios lead to see the importance of rapid and strong economic recovery effects. It is confirmed by the single debt explosion scenario when economic recovery does not reach the production potential of which crisis has alienated the global economy.

The last two scenarios, for their part, moderate concerns that sustained weaker potential growth raises about public finances' future. Without doubt we should observe that if a structural decline in potential growth rate does not disturb too much fiscal policy's long effects, it is largely because it was hypothesized that public expenditure in the short term move along with potential growth, simulations having a ratchet effect.

But these two scenarios' results also show that through fiscal policy's adaptability to potential growth terms, overestimating it did not affect public accounts too greatly. One might wish to prevent marginal effects that would imply, nevertheless, such an overestimation, by adopting an economic policy keyed on pessimistic prospects. But an overly cautious policy disadvantages more clearly than policy based on a more optimistic outlook.

Indeed, given the possible link between current fiscal policy and long-term growth, the risk of a too restrictive fiscal policy is to weaken the long term growth prospects. In addition, in shorter-term, we must remember that the more recovery is rapid and strong, the more public finances easily normalize, while adopting a very restrictive fiscal policy from the outset may "break" the recovery.

So the question is not whether international declarations, including from G-20, advocating maintenance of accommodative economic policies are relevant, but to know whether they will be implemented. In this context, two worrying matters: seeing the economic policies being broken and a speculation wave in the sovereign debt markets. On this second topic, Greece's example shows that market participants are beginning to distinguish between the Euro area States.

This situation is even more shocking in that some unsustainable fiscal positions come from the effects of a crisis triggered by imbalances resulting from these market participants' behavior. About the Greek episode's reproducibility, States should establish mechanisms preserving the chances of an orderly return to a stronger fiscal sustainability, which means needing to fight against speculation today.

Also, the world does not have a coordinated crisis program: if, so far, monetary policy has been accommodative, it would benefit if central banks stabilize over the long term agents' expectations by announcing the continuation of this policy.

Above all, it would take a G-world to undertake global economic policies coordination, without which the antagonisms may be unleashed again causing disastrous side effects, face to which States would find themselves helpless.

The crisis further amplifies the dangers of austerity fiscal policies. Let us highlight the unsustainability of unbalanced growth patterns, at the expense of labor and employees: the world in its current operation did not provide the assurances it should for a strong and sustainable growth. The crisis threatens more part of the workforce with employability since it generates strong and durable unemployment. Only the low growth scenario raised real global fiscal policy adequacy issue. It is important to focus on a global fiscal policy choice not likely to hasten the occurrence of this scenario.

In sum, public powers' interest towards global crisis, renewed global growth prospects, the recent dramatic advances in the global governance field are all assets to be finally forged Public Policies bearing hopes for the future.

However, despite some notable successes, the global economy suffers: jobs are lost, it regresses in terms of growth, and it ranks poorly in terms of the world's most innovative segments. But we cannot ignore it: countries will have their place in the world only by relying on sound and performing public finances. They will also find a way to create real jobs.

Thus beyond the necessary affirmation of the desire for better global governance, countries have a major role to play in this fight. Strongly aiming to global regulation must go hand in hand with great national ambition to settle fiscal imbalances: countries' handicaps - too much expenditure, too much tax, too much bureaucracy, we could add "excessive deficits" - require to be corrected.

BIBLIOGRAPHIE

- "Greenspan Concedes Error on Regulation", New York Times Accessed on 2009-04-18 nytimes.com
- Global inflation climbs to historic levels International Herald Tribune 12 February 2008 accessed on 11 July 2008
- "CIA Adds Economy To Threat Updates, White House Given First Daily Briefing" article by Joby Warrick, Washington Post Staff Writer, Thursday, February 26, 2009
- "Des États inégaux face au ralentissement mondial", Le Monde, 25 novembre 2008
- Massimo Calabresi, « Congress and the Bailout Plan: Business As Usual », dans Time Magazine, 23 septembre 2008.
- Personnel de rédaction, « Another shot in the arm », dans The Economist, 19 janvier 2009
- Bruno Birolli. Des milliards comme s'il en pleuvait ! Le Nouvel Obs, 21 novembre 2008
- ... et que donc la récession devrait prendre fin dans la plupart des pays. FMI : la croissance mondiale frôlera les 4 % en 2010, Le Figaro, 26 janvier 2010.
- Are emerging economies causing inflation? Economic Times (India) du 08/07/2008
- prospects-for-inflation-outside-america-guest-post-from-menzie-chinn/] Prospects for Inflation outside America - Guest Post from Menzie ChinnJeff Frankel's Weblog consulté le 11/07/20008
- Pierre de gasquet, « Les États-Unis officiellement en récession depuis décembre 2007 », Les Échos, 2/12/2008

- Peer Steinbrück on the Global Economic Crisis, Newsweek, 6 décembre 2008.
- « Relance ou dérive de la dette? Le dilemme des gouvernants face à la crise », dans Le Devoir, 24 janvier 2008
- Christian Chavagneux, Banques : des risques mal calculés, Alternatives économiques n°283 de septembre 2009, p.50
- Determination of the December 2007 Peak in Economic Activity, NBER, décembre 2008.
- Financial Transmission of the Crisis: What's the Lesson? Shimelse Ali, Uri Dadush, Lauren Falcao, "International Economics Bulletin, June 2009
- L'écrasante responsabilité des banquiers, Joseph Stiglitz, Le Nouvel Observateur, n°2365, 4 mars 2010.
- Pierre-Antoine Delhommais, "2009 : Rose bonbon gris foncé ou noir ?", Le Monde des 7 et 8 décembre 2008
- ZAGAT'S 2009 U.S. Hotels, resorts, & spas survey finds more options available for cost-conscious travelers, Zagat (2008-11-12).
- A Global Retreat As Economies Dry Up. The Washington Post. March 5, 2009.
- A juddering halt to world trade [archive]
- Managing the global financial crisis and economic downturn, OCDE, décembre 2008.
- Alain Faujas, Entretien avec Olivier Blanchard, Le Monde du 24/11/2009
- Alain Faujas, Selon le FMI, la récession mondiale s'achève, mais la reprise sera laborieuses, Le Monde du 2/10/2009

- Ann Pettifor, « America's financial meltdown: lessons and prospects », openDemocracy, 16 septembre 2008.
- Annie Kahn, Les Nouveaux "grands défis" de l'innovation aux États-Unis, Le Monde du 15/12/2009
- Brice Pedroletti, "L'afflux de liquidités provoque encore une flambée boursière à Hongkong et en Chine", Le Monde du 3/11/2009
- Bruno Ventelou in Alternatives économiques du 16 décembre 2008
- Business Week article "Economic Woes Raising Global Political Risk" by Jack Ewing published March 10, 2009
- Cécile Cornudet, "Nicolas Sarkozy répond à la crise économique par un effort public massif" Les Echos des 5 et 6 décembre 2008.
- China heads to Europe for a multi-billion trade deal. People's Daily Online. February 25, 2009.
- China, taking advantage of global recession, goes on a buying spree. The Christian Science Monitor. February 21, 2009
- Chinese sovereign fund turning to natural resources. Reuters. February 19, 2009.
- Christian Chavagneux, Banques : des risques mal calculés, Alternatives économiques n°283 de septembre 2009, p.51
- Christian Chavagneux, Banques : des risques mal calculés, Alternatives économiques n°283 de septembre 2009, p.52
- Citations précédentes extraites de l'entretien de Thierry de Montbrial avec Jean Christophe Floquin, La Croix du 27 février 2009
- Claire Gatinois, Le Monde, 3/11/2009

- Conjoncture : Obama prévoit un chômage élevé jusqu'en 2020, Le Figaro, 11 février 2010
- Daniel Cohen, "Du danger de croire que la crise économique est finie", Le Monde du 16 juin 2009
- Economic Crisis Poses Threat To Global Stability. NPR. February 18, 2009•
- Emploi et taux de chômage USA novembre 2010 : très mauvais Geocodia, décembre 2010
- Financial crisis to cost 20 mn jobs: UN
- Financial Transmission of the Crisis: What's the Lesson? Shimelse Ali, Uri Dadush, Lauren Falcao, "International Economics Bulletin, June 2009.
- Frédéric Lemaître Et si la crise économique ne faisait que commencer Le Monde du 7 juillet 2009
- Gabriel Grésillon, Les consommateurs chinois ne sauveront pas le monde, Les Échos des 23/24/10/2009
- Global unemployment heads towards 50 million, The Times, January 29, 2009
- Hélène Rey, « L'inévitable relance budgétaire », Les Échos du 20/11/2008
- Henry Gibier, "Copenhague, un lever de rideau", Les Échos, 5/11/2009
- HIGHLIGHTS: Crisis sends Japan into first recession in 7 years, Reuters, 2008-11-17.
- HK shares may fall; exporters may drop, Reuters, 2008-11-16.

- http://elections-americaines.lesechos.fr/article.php?id_article=2463
- http://lapresseaffaires.cyberpresse.ca/dossiers/pme/200901/06/01-691257-un-renfort-de-quebec-pour-les-entreprises.php
- http://lapresseaffaires.cyberpresse.ca/opinions/chroniques/richard-dupaul/200901/09/01-693360-chiche-ou-sage-angela-merkel.php
- http://tempsreel.nouvelobs.com/depeches/economie/20090113.REU4146/berlin_adopte_un_nouveau_plan_de_relance_de_50_milliard.html
- http://tempsreel.nouvelobs.com/depeches/economie/20090114.REU4278/un_plan_de_soutien_de_10_milliards_de_livres_aux_pme_an.html
- http://www.boursorama.com/international/detail_actu_intern.phtml?num=8d2331ba6e6235ff0f642ee8802048e4
- http://www.latribune.fr/actualites/economie/international/20081127trib000315037/madrid-annonce-un-plan-de-relance-de-11-milliards-deuros.html
- http://www.latribune.fr/actualites/economie/international/20090111trib000330123/plan-de-relance-barack-obama-prevoit-de-creer-entre-trois-et-quatre-millions-demplois.html
- http://www.lefigaro.fr/bourse/2010/01/25/04013-20100125ARTFIG00503-banques-le-debat-sur-la-regulation-financiere-relance-.php
- http://www.lefigaro.fr/international/2009/03/03/01003-20090303ARTFIG00007-gordon-brown-premier-invite-europeen-d-obama-.php

- http://www.lefigaro.fr/international/2010/01/10/01003-20100110ARTFIG00145-les-allemands-s-opposent-aux-baisses-d-impot-.php
- http://www.lejdd.fr/cmc/economie/200904/un-banquier-repond-a-sarkozy_182137.html
- http://www.lemonde.fr/economie/article/2009/03/01/gordon-brown-propose-un-new-deal-a-obama_1161869_3234.html
- http://www.lemonde.fr/europe/article/2009/01/19/londres-devoile-un-nouveau-plan-de-soutien-aux-banques_1143444_3214.html
- http://www.leparisien.fr/flash-actualite-economie/ocde-resorber-les-deficits-en-reduisant-le-chomage-et-certaines-depenses-10-03-2010-843091.php
- http://www.lepoint.fr/actualites-economie/2009-04-03/g20-compromis-historique-au-g20-pour-relancer-l-economie-et-reguler/916/0/331470
- http://www.lepoint.fr/actualites-economie/cent-milliards-de-couronnes-pour-relancer-le-credit-en-norvege/916/0/315085
- http://www.lesechos.fr/info/inter/300333887.htm
- http://www.lesechos.fr/info/inter/4805721.htm
- http://www.lesechos.fr/info/inter/afp_00223237-merkel-l-economie-allemande-ne-sera-pas-tiree-d-affaire-avant-2013.htm
- http://www.oecd.org/document/55/0,3343,fr_2649_34325_44758775_1_1_1_37443,00.html
- http://www.pcinpact.com/actu/news/48871-plan-relance-numerique-tgv-wifi.htm

- http://www.premier-ministre.gouv.fr/acteurs/communiques_4/premier_ministre_reuni_comite_62495.html
- http://www.premier-ministre.gouv.fr/chantiers/plan_relance_economie_1393/plan_relance_1_000_62486.html
- http://www.usinenouvelle.com/article/ocde-des-mesures-d-urgence-oui-mais-pas-sans-les-reformes.159812
- http://www.usinenouvelle.com/article/que-cache-le-debat-sur-le-protectionnisme.157737
- Isabelle Couet, Avec le retrait de la Réserve fédérale, le marché de la dette américaine perd un soutien de taille, Les Echos du 29/10/2009
- Jan Strupczewski, « Euro zone in recession, December rate cut expected », Reuters.com, 2008-11-14.
- Jean-Marc Vittori, "La finance publique revient au Moyen-Age", Les Échos, 12-13/02/2010
- Jean-Marc Vittori, "l'Amérique en fanfare", Les Échos des 30 et 31 octobre 2009
- Journal des Finances 10/02/2009 : Obama veut éviter une catastrophe
- Klaus Schmidt-Hebbel, Chef économiste de l'OCDE, « A long recession », OECD Observer, décembre 2008.
- Le Monde (11/11/08) : nationaliser les banques, une mauvaise solution
- Le Monde du 3//2009, "Question-réponses"

- Les citations viennent de traduction du rapport trouvé dans l'article d'Annie Kahn du 15/12/2009
- M. Fratianni et F. Marchionne, 2009, The Role of Banks in the Subprime Financial Crisis
- Marie-Laure Cittanova, Pour la France, le pire reste à venir, Les Echos des 17 et 18 septembre 2009
- Mari-Laure Cittanova, Impact de la crise dans les pays développés : 25 millions de chômeurs , selon l'OCDE, Les Echos du 17 septembre 2009
- Martin Walker, L'occident va devoir partager. Il nous faut inventer un autre modèle, Le Monde du 28 mars 2009
- Martin Wolf, Ce qu'Obama n'a pas dit à Hu, Les Échos du 24/11/2009
- Massimo Prandi, Newedge identifie la formation d'une nouvelle bulle sur les marchés, Les Échos du 21/10/2009
- National Bank estimate: Ukraine GDP down 20 percent in January, Kyiv Post, 2009-02-17.
- Nessim Aït-Kacimi, Pandémie sur les marchés financiers, Les Échos du 15/10/09
- New Zealand falls into recession [archive], BBC News, 2008-09-26.
- NPR article "Economic Crisis Poses Threat To Global Stability" by Tom Gjelten
- OECD area GDP down 0.1% in the third quarter of 2008, OECD, 2008-11-20.

- Organisation mondiale du tourisme, « UNWTO World Tourism Barometer October 2008 », OMT, October 2008. Volume 6, Issue 3
- Oxford Economic Country Briefings, « Latvia », Findarticles.com, September 26, 2008.
- Patrick Fitzgibbons, « TOPWRAP 10-Germany, China, US feel pain of global downturn », Reuters, 2008-11-14.
- Peer Steinbrück on the Global Economic Crisis, Newsweek, 6 décembre 2008.
- Pierre-Antoine Delhommais, Les G20 passent, l'horloge tourne Le Monde des 27 et 28 septembre 2009
- Polleit Thorsten, « Manipulating the Interest Rate: a Recipe for Disaster », Mises Institute, 2007-12-13.
- Presse Canadienne et AFP, 13 septembre 2008
- Rapport de l'OCDE : Objectif Croissance 2009, publié le 3 mars 2009.
- Reflating the dragon, The Economist, November 13, 2008.
- Richard Hiault « Pour le FMI, la reprise mondiale reste encore dépendante des plans de relance budgétaire » Les Echos du 27 janvier 2010
- Sandra Moatti, La mondialisation de la crise, Alternative économiques, n°275, décembre 2008, p.14
- Singapore slides into recession, Telegraph, 10 October 2008.
- Spain's economy enters recession, BBC News, 2009-01-28.
- Stefan Karlsson, « America's Unsustainable Boom », Mises Institute, 2004-11-08.

- Strange rise of Eastern neo-colonialism, The Times of India, January 20, 2008
- Christian Walter et Michel de Pracontal, Le Virus B "crise financière et mathématiques,
- Sweden stumbles into recession, The Local, 2008-11-28.
- Sylvain Cypel, Aux États-Unis, le chômage a atteint son plus haut niveau depuis vingt-six ans, Le Monde des 8 et 9 novembre 2009
- Taiwan in recession, 2009-02-18. Consulté le 2009-04-10
- The Associated Press article "Experts: Financial crisis threatens US security" by Stephen Manning, publié le 11 mars 2009
- Virginie Malingre, "Grodon Brown est contraint de renoncer à un nouveau plan de relance, Le Monde du 27 mars 2009
- Virginie Robert, "L'économie encore trop fragile pour que la Fed modifie ses taux" Les Échos du 5/11/2009
- Virginie Robert, La Banque mondiale annonce une croissance chinoise à 8,4 % cette année" Les Échos du 5/11/2009
- Claire Gatinois, le Monde du 3/11/209
- What Went Wrong, The Washington Post, 2008-10-15.
- Whitney Mike, « Stock Market Meltdown », Global Research, 6 août 2007.
- Yann Rousseau, " Dans la crise, la Chine a renforcé son influence sur l'Afrique" Les Échos des 6 et 7 novembre 2009.
- Yann Rousseau, Beaucoup de promesses d'entente peu d'engagements concrets Les Echos du 18/11/2009.

- Yann Rousseau, Le directeur du FMI presse Pékin de réévaluer le yuan Les Échos du 18/11/2009
- a et b Marie Verdier, Le déclin du pétrole a-t-il commencé ?, La croix, 27 January 2009; p.14
- Bruegel (think tank), *Estimating the size off the stimulus package for 2009*, 12 December 2008
- CIBC World Markets date: May 27, 2008 accessed on 2009-01-04.
- David Lightman Congressional Budget Office compares downturn to Great Depression, McClatchy Washington Bureau. January 27, 2009.
- Dupret X, 2009, "Krach mondial", Ed. Couleurs Livres.
- Evans-Pritchard, Ambrose : With the US trapped in depression, this really is starting to feel like 1932, The Daily Telegraph (2010-07-04).
- Fredric S. Mishkin, How Should We Respond to Asset Price Bubbles? Accessed on 2008-04-18
- George A. Akerlof et Robert Shiller, 2009, *Les esprits animaux : comment les forces psychologiques mènent la finance et l'économie*, Pearson
- Inequality and depression: Ravi Batra's original thesis on financial crisis published on 1987-09-27 in Forbes
- Krugman P., 2009, *Pourquoi les crises reviennent toujours* , Editions du Seuil, Paris.
- Les deux chiffres précédents viennent de l'article de Yves Bourdillon, Les Nations unies redoutent une nette aggravation de la crise alimentaire, Les Echos, 2009-01-27

- Light Crude Oil EmiNY (QM, NYMEX): Monthly Price Chart Tfc-charts.com [archive] accessed on 2009-01-04.
- Massimo Prandi, Les produits agricoles échapperont seuls à la récession, selon CyclOpe, Les Echos, 2009-01-29
- Michel de Pracontal et Christian Walter *Le virus B. Crises financières et mathématiques,* Ed. du Seuil, 2009, 127 p.
- Nouriel Roubini A Global Breakdown of The Recession In 2009, January 15, 2009.
- Pierre-Antoine Delhommais, «Bulles, bulles, bulles» Le Monde, 2010-01-31 & 2010-02-01
- Rampell, Catherine : The 'Great Recession' Earns Its Title, The New York Times (2010-07-30).
- Richard Hiault «Pour le FMI, la reprise mondiale reste encore dépendante des plans de relance budgétaire» Les Echos, 27 January 2010.
- Servet, J-M., 2010, *De la crise au renouveau solidaire*, Desclée de Brouwer, Paris.
- Wearden Graeme, Oil prices: George Soros warns that speculators could trigger stock market 06/03/2008 The Guardian.
- Zuckerman, Mortimer : Mortimer Zuckerman: The Great Recession Continues - WSJ.com, Online.wsj.com Accessed on 2010-05-01.

www.ingramcontent.com/pod-product-compliance
Lightning Source LLC
LaVergne TN
LVHW020412220926
848484LV00016B/2551/J
* 9 7 8 0 9 8 2 8 4 3 4 9 9 *